1992

PERSONAL BIBLE STUDY ❦ JOURNAL

*Your word is a lamp
to my feet and a
light for my path.*

World Wide Publications
Minneapolis, Minnesota 55403

1992 Personal Bible Study Journal

© 1991 by World Wide Publications

World Wide Publications is the publishing ministry of the Billy Graham Evangelistic Association.

Unless otherwise indicated, Scripture quotations are taken from The Holy Bible, New International Version. © 1973, 1978, 1984 International Bible Society. Used by permission of Zondervan Bible Publishers.

Scripture quotations marked NASB are taken from the New American Standard Bible, © 1960, 1962, 1963, 1968, 1971, 1972, 1973, 1975, 1977 The Lockman Foundation, La Habra, California.

ISBN: 0-89066-215-0

Printed in the United States of America

Contents

"Your Word Is Truth"

"Your word is truth." Jesus prayed those words to God just hours before his crucifixion (John 17:17). It was a time of great concern for our Lord. He had worked with his disciples for three years and was now shortly to be taken from them. But he could leave confident that a foundation of truth had been laid for their ministry through his Father's spoken and written word.

Down through the ages Christians have echoed Christ's certainty amid the various uncertainties of life. "Your word is truth" they whisper as children leave home with graduation Bibles and memories of family devotions. Facing times of grief or trial, they turn to God's everlasting words of comfort. Facing important life decisions they consult all the "expert opinions," then go to the one source that is more than just opinion.

"Your word is truth," Jesus says; and just forty-seven verses later Pilate contemptuously asks, "What is truth?" (18:38). His words, too, have been echoed down through time, either by people who don't want their evil deeds exposed to the light of truth, or by those who have honestly concluded that truth cannot be known.

In America and many other Christian nations, there is a third group, a "silent majority" between the students and detractors of God's Word. These are people who say they believe in God's Word, but who rarely open its covers.

As you open the pages of this ***Personal Bible Study Journal***, you may find yourself in one of these categories— already a student of the Bible; skeptical that truth can really be found, but willing to give the Bible a try; or simply making one more effort to become acquainted with the book you've always said you believe in. Whichever category you are in, you have taken the first step. You have said, I *will* make an effort this year to learn more about the Bible.

We commend you as you begin your year with God's Word. You'll want to read the tips for effective Bible study on the following pages. And unless you already have a plan in place, you should try to follow the "One-Year Bible Survey" on pages 121–176.

As 1992 draws to a close, may you say with all your heart, "Your word is truth."

Some How-to's for Personal Bible Study

Our goal in personal Bible study is to internalize the Word of God, allowing it to change our lives. In order to do that, we must understand how its original message affects us in the twentieth century. We are not looking for some hidden meaning in Scripture. Rather, we are seeking to comprehend its *obvious* meaning—the meaning in the mind of the writer and, ultimately, in the mind of God.

Here are some methods for discovering the clear meaning of a Scripture passage:

1. Ask Questions of the Passage

Who. Who is present in the passage? (And who is *not* present?) Who is speaking? Who is listening?

What. What is happening? What is the outcome? What *might* have happened?

Where. Where did the action occur? Where had they been? Where were they going?

When. When in history did the action occur? At what period in the lives of the people involved did it occur?

Why. Why did this occur? Why was this said?

How. How did each person feel about what occurred or what was said? Why did they feel that way?

Asking such simple questions is an effective way of *meditating* on God's Word (Psalm 1:2). Such questions force us to bring Scripture into the realm of human emotion and experience—and hopefully to apply what we discover to our own emotions and experience.

2. Look for Key Words

Verbs. The "action" words in the Bible often contain food for thought and meditation. What does Paul mean, for instance, when he tells us to "put to death" certain things in our lives, or to "set your mind on" certain other things?

Connectors. Words that unite thoughts are the easiest to miss. "Therefore," "but," "in order that," "since," "yet," "so," and "because" are some of the more important connectors. These tiny words unite large ideas, much like small couplings on railroad cars hold a train together. A word's importance can never be judged by its size, especially in the Bible. For instance, the first and most important word in the twelfth chapter of Romans is "therefore."

Repeated words or phrases. An author will often emphasize a point by repeating certain words or phrases. As we study a particular passage, we should be attentive for a word or series of words that is used more than once.

3. Compare and Contrast

Comparison. Determine how two things, persons, or ideas in a Scripture text are similar. Words or phrases like "just as," "likewise," "in the same way," or "even so" can be clues that a comparison is being made. Why is the author making a comparison?

Contrast. It is also important to note when two things, persons, or ideas are *different*. Again, connecting words provide the clue: "rather," "but," "not," "neither . . . nor," or "however."

Noticing comparisons and contrasts will open new vistas in chapters like Romans 5, where Jesus is compared with Adam, and Hebrews 7, where his priesthood is contrasted with the priesthood of Melchizedek.

4. Isolate the Units of Study

Don't be misled by the chapter and verse divisions in our English translations. Such divisions did not occur in the original manuscripts, and they often interrupt the flow of thought. It is safer to base your study on paragraph divisions. When a new paragraph begins, the author is changing his line of thought, or adding to previous ideas or arguments.

Many English translations add subheads to groups of one or more paragraphs. For instance, the *New International Version* breaks Romans 9:1–29 into eight paragraphs and gives it the subhead, "God's Sovereign Choice." While subheads, like chapter and verse divisions, are not part of the inspired text of Scripture, they can help readers organize their study.

5. Outline and Title

After becoming aware of the paragraphs and subheads added by the people who translated your Bible, you may want to try adding your own "personalized" subheads. First try titling each paragraph, then groups of paragraphs, then entire chapters.

6. Be Aware of the Context

One of the most important rules for Bible study is the rule of context. We can misunderstand what an author is saying simply by neglecting to read the surrounding verses. For example, Paul says in 1 Corinthians 2:9, "No eye has seen, no ear has heard, no mind has conceived what God has prepared for those who love Him" (NASB). Does Paul mean that the things God has prepared are totally beyond our understanding? No, because in the very next verse he continues, "But God has revealed it to us through the Spirit."

The rule of context simply means that we need to study a verse in its surroundings. Sometimes, of course, we may need to consider the context of an entire book or even of the entire Bible, in order to understand one verse. For instance, when Paul says "work out your salvation" (Philippians 2:12), is he preaching salvation by works? A look at the surrounding verses, then at the larger context of Philippians and Paul's other writings, and finally at the Bible as a whole, assures us that Paul is saying no such thing.

7. Use Different Versions of the Bible

One of the easiest ways to increase your understanding of a passage of Scripture is to compare how it reads in different Bible versions. Note especially the various translations of key words. Try writing out the verse incorporating all the different translations of those key words.

These seven tools will not fit every passage you study, any more than a hammer or screwdriver can be used for every home project. But when you do use them, you will discover a whole new world opening up between the covers of your Bible.

Making a Personal Application

The most valuable result of daily Bible study is not the acquisition of more Bible knowledge, but the awareness that your life is being changed and enriched through the personal application of what you learn. Following is a sample "personal application plan":

1. **Verse.** Record the verse or passage which you want to apply to your own life.

2. **Truth.** Briefly state in your own words the truth of that verse or passage.

3. **Need.** State how you feel you fall short in relation to the truth of the passage.

4. **Intent.** State specifically what you intend to do toward having your life changed in this area of need. Keep the action simple. It should be just one step toward improving your life in this area.

5. **Checkup.** State how you will make sure you accomplish the simple goal you have set. You may want to jot a note and put it somewhere in your office or home where you'll see it often until you have completed your application. You may want to tell a friend, your husband or wife, or another relative what you intend to do, so that they can check up on you.

Example:

1. **Verse.** "Be devoted to one another in brotherly love. Honor one another above yourselves" (Romans 12:10).

2. **Truth.** That God wants me to show devotion and honor to my brothers and sisters in Christ.

3. **Need.** I find I often take my closer relationships with other Christians for granted. I seldom think about ways to honor them and be devoted to them. Dan is one person I particularly want to honor more.

4. **Intent.** I will spend Saturday helping Dan finish painting his house, and while we talk I will make a point of specifically complimenting him about at least two things I respect about him.

5. **Checkup.** I will place a check mark here ☐ Saturday night after I have done this.

What God Has Written to *You*

God has written only one book—the Bible. Of the millions of books that have been written, it alone deserves to be called "the Book." The Bible offers eternal life to everyone who heeds its invitation, and spiritual food for Christians growing in the Lord. So it should be no surprise to us that this book continues to be the most-read of all books. People of all lands and languages sense a strong attachment to it. What a priceless privilege and opportunity to read what God has written to us!*

Reading the Bible every day should be a natural, unforced activity in your walk with God. Here are some practical suggestions for making these times more fruitful:

- The length of reading may be short or long. Variety is good. Spend time reflecting on what you have read.

- Choose the time of day when you are most alert, wide awake, least rushed, and most able to concentrate.

- Establish your own regular pattern of reading, as a guard against distractions and detours.

- Read the Bible text carefully, prayerfully, repeatedly, aloud at times, humbly, and expectantly. Read to learn what God has written to *you*.

- Look to the Holy Spirit, who can guide and inspire you as you read.

—*Irving L. Jensen*

*From Irving L. Jensen, *Simply Understanding the Bible* (Minneapolis: World Wide Publications, 1990), 7.

Journal Pages

The "One-Year Bible Survey" beginning on page 119 is designed to guide you through key passages in the Bible in one year's time. You will notice there are seven passages presented on each page, one for each day of the week. There are also some questions on each passage, designed simply to "get the ball rolling" as you dig into the passage and discover what God is saying personally to you. (Many chapters and even some entire books have been omitted to fit the short-daily-reading format. Don't hesitate to fill in those gaps if you have the time!)

You can then record what you learn from each passage on the following calendar pages. For each day there is a place to record: (1) *My Thoughts:* Use this space to answer the questions for each day and to record how God spoke to you personally through his Word; (2) *My Application:* This is the most important part of your daily Bible study! How will what you read today make a difference in how you live today? Try to think of at least one "action step" you can take to apply what you have just learned.

The "One-Year Bible Survey" can easily be adapted for use in church or home group Bible study settings. Each student should study the passages personally each day of the week. Then, on Sunday, the whole class can compare notes on what God taught them that week.

Here's an example of how you might fill in one page of your ***Personal Bible Study Journal:***

28 Saturday

Passage _John 3:1-21_

My Thoughts: _Nicodemus seems to be sincerely seeking. Jesus was very direct in his answers; seems to be a firm line between those who believe and those who don't_

My Application: _I wonder if some of my friends are seeking truth but are afraid to ask._

JANUARY

S	M	T	W	T	F	S
			1	2	3	4
5	6	7	8	9	10	11
12	13	14	15	16	17	18
19	20	21	22	23	24	25
26	27	28	29	30	31	

29 Sunday

Passage _______________________

My Thoughts: ____

____

____

____

My Application: ______________________________________

____

____

30 Monday

Passage _______________________

My Thoughts: ____

____

____

____

My Application: ______________________________________

____

____

31 Tuesday

Passage _______________________

My Thoughts: ____

____

____

My Application: ______________________________________

____

____

1 Wednesday

Passage _______________________

My Thoughts: _______________________
____
____
____

My Application: _______________________
____
____

2 Thursday

Passage _______________________

My Thoughts: _______________________
____
____
____

My Application: _______________________
____
____

3 Friday

Passage _______________________

My Thoughts: _______________________
____
____
____

My Application: _______________________
____
____

4 Saturday

Passage _______________________

My Thoughts: _______________________
____
____
____

My Application: _______________________
____
____

January

5 Sunday

Passage _______________________

My Thoughts: _______________________________________

____

____

____

My Application: ____________________________________

____

____

6 Monday

Passage _______________________

My Thoughts: _______________________________________

____

____

____

My Application: ____________________________________

____

____

7 Tuesday

Passage _______________________

My Thoughts: _______________________________________

____

____

____

My Application: ____________________________________

____

____

8 Wednesday

Passage ___________________________

My Thoughts: ___________________________

____

____

____

My Application: ___________________________

____

____

9 Thursday

Passage ___________________________

My Thoughts: ___________________________

____

____

____

My Application: ___________________________

____

____

10 Friday

Passage ___________________________

My Thoughts: ___________________________

____

____

____

My Application: ___________________________

____

____

11 Saturday

Passage ___________________________

My Thoughts: ___________________________

____

____

____

My Application: ___________________________

____

____

JANUARY

S	M	T	W	T	F	S
			1	2	3	4
5	6	7	8	9	10	11
12	13	14	15	16	17	18
19	20	21	22	23	24	25
26	27	28	29	30	31	

12 Sunday

Passage _______________________

My Thoughts: ____

____

____

____

My Application: ______________________________________

____

____

13 Monday

Passage _______________________

My Thoughts: ____

____

____

____

My Application: ______________________________________

____

____

14 Tuesday

Passage _______________________

My Thoughts: ____

____

____

____

My Application: ______________________________________

____

____

15 Wednesday

Passage ___________________

My Thoughts: ____

____

____

My Application: ____

____

____

16 Thursday

Passage ___________________

My Thoughts: ____

____

____

My Application: ____

____

____

17 Friday

Passage ___________________

My Thoughts: ____

____

____

My Application: ____

____

____

18 Saturday

Passage ___________________

My Thoughts: ____

____

My Application: ____

____

____

JANUARY

S	M	T	W	T	F	S
			1	2	3	4
5	6	7	8	9	10	11
12	13	14	15	16	17	18
19	20	21	22	23	24	25
26	27	28	29	30	31	

19 Sunday

Passage ___________________

My Thoughts: ____

____

____

____

My Application: ____

____

____

20 Monday

Passage ___________________

My Thoughts: ____

____

____

____

My Application: ____

____

____

21 Tuesday

Passage ___________________

My Thoughts: ____

____

____

____

My Application: ____

____

____

22 Wednesday

Passage ________________

My Thoughts: ____

____

____

My Application: _____________________________________

____

____

23 Thursday

Passage ________________

My Thoughts: ____

____

____

My Application: _____________________________________

____

____

24 Friday

Passage ________________

My Thoughts: ____

____

____

My Application: _____________________________________

____

____

25 Saturday

Passage ________________

My Thoughts: ____

____

____

My Application: _____________________________________

____

____

JANUARY

S	M	T	W	T	F	S
			1	2	3	4
5	6	7	8	9	10	11
12	13	14	15	16	17	18
19	20	21	22	23	24	25
26	27	28	29	30	31	

26 Sunday

Passage _______________

My Thoughts: _______________________________________

____

____

____

My Application: ____________________________________

____

____

27 Monday

Passage _______________

My Thoughts: _______________________________________

____

____

____

My Application: ____________________________________

____

____

28 Tuesday

Passage _______________

My Thoughts: _______________________________________

____

____

____

My Application: ____________________________________

____

____

29 Wednesday

Passage _______________________

My Thoughts: ____

____

____

____

My Application: ____

____

____

30 Thursday

Passage _______________________

My Thoughts: ____

____

____

____

My Application: ____

____

____

31 Friday

Passage _______________________

My Thoughts: ____

____

____

____

My Application: ____

____

____

1 Saturday

Passage _______________________

My Thoughts: ____

____

____

My Application: ____

____

____

February

2 Sunday

Passage _______________

My Thoughts: _______________________________

____

____

____

My Application: _____________________________

____

____

3 Monday

Passage _______________

My Thoughts: _______________________________

____

____

____

My Application: _____________________________

____

____

4 Tuesday

Passage _______________

My Thoughts: _______________________________

____

____

____

My Application: _____________________________

____

____

5 Wednesday

Passage ___________________

My Thoughts: ___________________

____

____

My Application: ___________________

____

6 Thursday

Passage ___________________

My Thoughts: ___________________

____

____

My Application: ___________________

____

7 Friday

Passage ___________________

My Thoughts: ___________________

____

____

My Application: ___________________

____

8 Saturday

Passage ___________________

My Thoughts: ___________________

____

____

My Application: ___________________

____

February

February 1992

S	M	T	W	T	F	S
						1
2	3	4	5	6	7	8
9	10	11	12	13	14	15
16	17	18	19	20	21	22
23	24	25	26	27	28	29

9 Sunday

Passage _______________________

My Thoughts: _______________________________________

My Application: ___________________________________

10 Monday

Passage _______________________

My Thoughts: _______________________________________

My Application: ___________________________________

11 Tuesday

Passage _______________________

My Thoughts: _______________________________________

My Application: ___________________________________

12 Wednesday

Passage ___________________________

My Thoughts: ___________________________

____

____

____

My Application: ___________________________

____

____

13 Thursday

Passage ___________________________

My Thoughts: ___________________________

____

____

____

My Application: ___________________________

____

____

14 Friday

Passage ___________________________

My Thoughts: ___________________________

____

____

____

My Application: ___________________________

____

____

15 Saturday

Passage ___________________________

My Thoughts: ___________________________

____

____

____

My Application: ___________________________

____

____

FEBRUARY

16 Sunday

Passage _______________________

My Thoughts: ____

____

____

____

My Application: ____

____

____

17 Monday

Passage _______________________

My Thoughts: ____

____

____

____

My Application: ____

____

____

18 Tuesday

Passage _______________________

My Thoughts: ____

____

____

____

My Application: ____

____

____

19 Wednesday

Passage _______________________

My Thoughts: _______________________

____

____

____

My Application: _______________________

____

____

20 Thursday

Passage _______________________

My Thoughts: _______________________

____

____

____

My Application: _______________________

____

____

21 Friday

Passage _______________________

My Thoughts: _______________________

____

____

____

My Application: _______________________

____

____

22 Saturday

Passage _______________________

My Thoughts: _______________________

____

____

____

My Application: _______________________

____

____

FEBRUARY

S	M	T	W	T	F	S
						1
2	3	4	5	6	7	8
9	10	11	12	13	14	15
16	17	18	19	20	21	22
23	24	25	26	27	28	29

23 Sunday

Passage _______________________

My Thoughts: _______________________________________

____

____

____

My Application: ___________________________________

____

____

24 Monday

Passage _______________________

My Thoughts: _______________________________________

____

____

____

My Application: ___________________________________

____

____

25 Tuesday

Passage _______________________

My Thoughts: _______________________________________

____

____

My Application: ___________________________________

____

____

26 Wednesday

Passage _______________

My Thoughts: _______________

____

____

____

My Application: _______________

____

____

27 Thursday

Passage _______________

My Thoughts: _______________

____

____

____

My Application: _______________

____

____

28 Friday

Passage _______________

My Thoughts: _______________

____

____

____

My Application: _______________

____

____

29 Saturday

Passage _______________

My Thoughts: _______________

____

____

____

My Application: _______________

____

____

MARCH

1 Sunday

Passage _______________________

My Thoughts: _______________________

____

____

____

My Application: _______________________

____

____

2 Monday

Passage _______________________

My Thoughts: _______________________

____

____

____

My Application: _______________________

____

____

3 Tuesday

Passage _______________________

My Thoughts: _______________________

____

____

____

My Application: _______________________

____

____

4 Wednesday

Passage _______________

My Thoughts: _______________

____

____

My Application: _______________

____

5 Thursday

Passage _______________

My Thoughts: _______________

____

____

My Application: _______________

____

6 Friday

Passage _______________

My Thoughts: _______________

____

____

My Application: _______________

____

7 Saturday

Passage _______________

My Thoughts: _______________

____

____

My Application: _______________

____

MARCH

8 Sunday

Passage _______________________

My Thoughts: _______________________

____

____

____

My Application: _______________________

____

____

9 Monday

Passage _______________________

My Thoughts: _______________________

____

____

____

My Application: _______________________

____

____

10 Tuesday

Passage _______________________

My Thoughts: _______________________

____

____

My Application: _______________________

____

____

11 Wednesday

Passage _______________________

My Thoughts: _______________________

____

____

____

My Application: _______________________

____

____

12 Thursday

Passage _______________________

My Thoughts: _______________________

____

____

____

My Application: _______________________

____

____

13 Friday

Passage _______________________

My Thoughts: _______________________

____

____

____

My Application: _______________________

____

____

14 Saturday

Passage _______________________

My Thoughts: _______________________

____

____

____

My Application: _______________________

____

____

MARCH

15 Sunday

Passage _______________

My Thoughts: ____

____

____

____

My Application: ____

____

____

16 Monday

Passage _______________

My Thoughts: ____

____

____

____

My Application: ____

____

____

17 Tuesday

Passage _______________

My Thoughts: ____

____

____

____

My Application: ____

____

____

18 Wednesday

Passage _______________

My Thoughts: ____

____

____

My Application: ______________________________________

____

____

19 Thursday

Passage _______________

My Thoughts: ____

____

____

My Application: ______________________________________

____

____

20 Friday

Passage _______________

My Thoughts: ____

____

____

My Application: ______________________________________

____

____

21 Saturday

Passage _______________

My Thoughts: ____

____

____

My Application: ______________________________________

____

____

MARCH

22 Sunday

Passage ___________________

My Thoughts: ____

____

____

____

My Application: ____

____

____

23 Monday

Passage ___________________

My Thoughts: ____

____

____

____

My Application: ____

____

____

24 Tuesday

Passage ___________________

My Thoughts: ____

____

____

____

My Application: ____

____

____

25 Wednesday

Passage _______________________

My Thoughts: _______________________
____
____
____

My Application: _______________________
____
____

26 Thursday

Passage _______________________

My Thoughts: _______________________
____
____
____

My Application: _______________________
____
____

27 Friday

Passage _______________________

My Thoughts: _______________________
____
____
____

My Application: _______________________
____
____

28 Saturday

Passage _______________________

My Thoughts: _______________________
____
____
____

My Application: _______________________
____
____

MARCH

29 Sunday

Passage _______________________

My Thoughts: ____

____

____

____

My Application: _______________________________________

____

____

30 Monday

Passage _______________________

My Thoughts: ____

____

____

____

My Application: _______________________________________

____

____

31 Tuesday

Passage _______________________

My Thoughts: ____

____

____

____

My Application: _______________________________________

____

____

1 Wednesday

Passage _______________________

My Thoughts: ____

____

____

My Application: ____

____

____

2 Thursday

Passage _______________________

My Thoughts: ____

____

____

My Application: ____

____

____

3 Friday

Passage _______________________

My Thoughts: ____

____

____

My Application: ____

____

____

4 Saturday

Passage _______________________

My Thoughts: ____

____

____

My Application: ____

____

____

APRIL

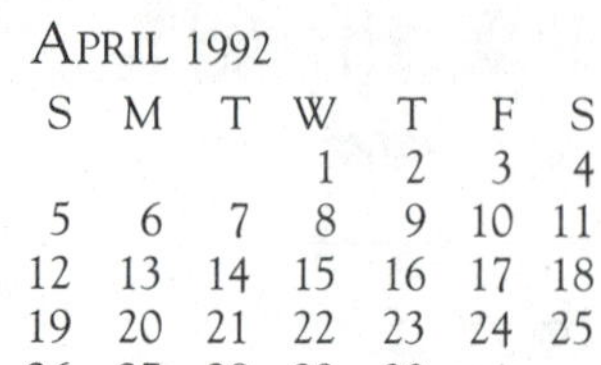

5 Sunday

Passage _______________________

My Thoughts: _______________________

____

____

My Application: _______________________

____

____

6 Monday

Passage _______________________

My Thoughts: _______________________

____

____

My Application: _______________________

____

____

7 Tuesday

Passage _______________________

My Thoughts: _______________________

____

My Application: _______________________

____

8 Wednesday

Passage _______________________

My Thoughts: _______________________

____

____

____

My Application: _______________________

____

____

9 Thursday

Passage _______________________

My Thoughts: _______________________

____

____

____

My Application: _______________________

____

____

10 Friday

Passage _______________________

My Thoughts: _______________________

____

____

____

My Application: _______________________

____

____

11 Saturday

Passage _______________________

My Thoughts: _______________________

____

____

____

My Application: _______________________

____

____

APRIL

12 Sunday

Passage ___________________

My Thoughts: ___________________
____
____
____

My Application: ___________________
____
____

13 Monday

Passage ___________________

My Thoughts: ___________________
____
____
____

My Application: ___________________
____
____

14 Tuesday

Passage ___________________

My Thoughts: ___________________
____
____

My Application: ___________________
____
____

15 Wednesday

Passage _______________________

My Thoughts: _______________________

____

____

My Application: _______________________

____

16 Thursday

Passage _______________________

My Thoughts: _______________________

____

____

My Application: _______________________

____

17 Friday

Passage _______________________

My Thoughts: _______________________

____

____

My Application: _______________________

____

18 Saturday

Passage _______________________

My Thoughts: _______________________

____

____

My Application: _______________________

____

APRIL

19 Sunday

Passage _______________________

My Thoughts: ____

____

____

____

My Application: ____

____

____

20 Monday

Passage _______________________

My Thoughts: ____

____

____

____

My Application: ____

____

____

21 Tuesday

Passage _______________________

My Thoughts: ____

____

____

____

My Application: ____

____

____

22 Wednesday

Passage _____________________

My Thoughts: _____________________

____

____

____

My Application: _____________________

____

____

23 Thursday

Passage _____________________

My Thoughts: _____________________

____

____

____

My Application: _____________________

____

____

24 Friday

Passage _____________________

My Thoughts: _____________________

____

____

____

My Application: _____________________

____

____

25 Saturday

Passage _____________________

My Thoughts: _____________________

____

____

____

My Application: _____________________

____

____

APRIL

S	M	T	W	T	F	S
			1	2	3	4
5	6	7	8	9	10	11
12	13	14	15	16	17	18
19	20	21	22	23	24	25
26	27	28	29	30		

26 Sunday

Passage _______________

My Thoughts: _______________________________

____

____

____

My Application: _______________________________

____

____

27 Monday

Passage _______________

My Thoughts: _______________________________

____

____

____

My Application: _______________________________

____

____

28 Tuesday

Passage _______________

My Thoughts: _______________________________

____

____

____

My Application: _______________________________

____

____

29 Wednesday

Passage ____________________

My Thoughts: ______________________________

____

____

____

My Application: ______________________________

____

____

30 Thursday

Passage ____________________

My Thoughts: ______________________________

____

____

____

My Application: ______________________________

____

____

1 Friday

Passage ____________________

My Thoughts: ______________________________

____

____

____

My Application: ______________________________

____

____

2 Saturday

Passage ____________________

My Thoughts: ______________________________

____

____

My Application: ______________________________

____

____

MAY

3 Sunday

Passage _______________________

My Thoughts: _______________________
____
____
____

My Application: _______________________
____
____

4 Monday

Passage _______________________

My Thoughts: _______________________
____
____
____

My Application: _______________________
____
____

5 Tuesday

Passage _______________________

My Thoughts: _______________________
____
____
____

My Application: _______________________
____
____

6 Wednesday

Passage ___________________

My Thoughts: ___________________

____

____

____

My Application: ___________________

____

____

7 Thursday

Passage ___________________

My Thoughts: ___________________

____

____

____

My Application: ___________________

____

____

8 Friday

Passage ___________________

My Thoughts: ___________________

____

____

____

My Application: ___________________

____

____

9 Saturday

Passage ___________________

My Thoughts: ___________________

____

____

____

My Application: ___________________

____

____

MAY

S	M	T	W	T	F	S
					1	2
3	4	5	6	7	8	9
10	11	12	13	14	15	16
17	18	19	20	21	22	23
24	25	26	27	28	29	30
31						

10 Sunday

Passage _______________________

My Thoughts: _______________________

____

____

____

My Application: _______________________

____

____

11 Monday

Passage _______________________

My Thoughts: _______________________

____

____

____

My Application: _______________________

____

____

12 Tuesday

Passage _______________________

My Thoughts: _______________________

____

____

____

My Application: _______________________

____

____

13 Wednesday

Passage ______________________

My Thoughts: ___________________________________

____

____

____

My Application: _________________________________

____

____

14 Thursday

Passage ______________________

My Thoughts: ___________________________________

____

____

____

My Application: _________________________________

____

____

15 Friday

Passage ______________________

My Thoughts: ___________________________________

____

____

____

My Application: _________________________________

____

____

16 Saturday

Passage ______________________

My Thoughts: ___________________________________

____

____

My Application: _________________________________

____

____

MAY

17 Sunday

Passage ______________________

My Thoughts: ______________________

____

____

____

My Application: ______________________

____

____

18 Monday

Passage ______________________

My Thoughts: ______________________

____

____

____

My Application: ______________________

____

____

19 Tuesday

Passage ______________________

My Thoughts: ______________________

____

____

____

My Application: ______________________

____

____

20 Wednesday

Passage ___________________

My Thoughts: ___________________

____

____

____

My Application: ___________________

____

____

21 Thursday

Passage ___________________

My Thoughts: ___________________

____

____

____

My Application: ___________________

____

____

22 Friday

Passage ___________________

My Thoughts: ___________________

____

____

____

My Application: ___________________

____

____

23 Saturday

Passage ___________________

My Thoughts: ___________________

____

____

____

My Application: ___________________

____

____

MAY

MAY 1992

S	M	T	W	T	F	S
					1	2
3	4	5	6	7	8	9
10	11	12	13	14	15	16
17	18	19	20	21	22	23
24	25	26	27	28	29	30
31						

24 Sunday

Passage ________________

My Thoughts: ____

____

____

____

My Application: ______________________________________

____

____

25 Monday

Passage ________________

My Thoughts: ____

____

____

____

My Application: ______________________________________

____

____

26 Tuesday

Passage ________________

My Thoughts: ____

____

____

____

My Application: ______________________________________

____

____

27 Wednesday

Passage _______________________

My Thoughts: _______________________

My Application: _______________________

28 Thursday

Passage _______________________

My Thoughts: _______________________

My Application: _______________________

29 Friday

Passage _______________________

My Thoughts: _______________________

My Application: _______________________

30 Saturday

Passage _______________________

My Thoughts: _______________________

My Application: _______________________

JUNE

S	M	T	W	T	F	S
	1	2	3	4	5	6
7	8	9	10	11	12	13
14	15	16	17	18	19	20
21	22	23	24	25	26	27
28	29	30				

31 Sunday

Passage ___________________

My Thoughts: ____

____

____

____

My Application: ____

____

____

1 Monday

Passage ___________________

My Thoughts: ____

____

____

____

My Application: ____

____

____

2 Tuesday

Passage ___________________

My Thoughts: ____

____

____

My Application: ____

____

3 Wednesday

Passage ________________

My Thoughts: ________________

____

____

____

My Application: ________________

____

____

4 Thursday

Passage ________________

My Thoughts: ________________

____

____

____

My Application: ________________

____

____

5 Friday

Passage ________________

My Thoughts: ________________

____

____

____

My Application: ________________

____

____

6 Saturday

Passage ________________

My Thoughts: ________________

____

____

____

My Application: ________________

____

____

JUNE

S	M	T	W	T	F	S
	1	2	3	4	5	6
7	8	9	10	11	12	13
14	15	16	17	18	19	20
21	22	23	24	25	26	27
28	29	30				

7 Sunday

Passage _______________

My Thoughts: _______________

____

____

____

My Application: _______________

____

____

8 Monday

Passage _______________

My Thoughts: _______________

____

____

____

My Application: _______________

____

____

9 Tuesday

Passage _______________

My Thoughts: _______________

____

____

____

My Application: _______________

____

____

10 Wednesday

Passage _______________

My Thoughts: _______________

____

____

My Application: _______________

____

11 Thursday

Passage _______________

My Thoughts: _______________

____

____

My Application: _______________

____

12 Friday

Passage _______________

My Thoughts: _______________

____

____

My Application: _______________

____

13 Saturday

Passage _______________

My Thoughts: _______________

____

____

My Application: _______________

____

JUNE

JUNE 1992

S	M	T	W	T	F	S
		1	2	3	4	5	6
7	8	9	10	11	12	13
14	15	16	17	18	19	20
21	22	23	24	25	26	27
28	29	30				

14 Sunday

Passage _______________

My Thoughts: _______________
____
____
____

My Application: _______________
____
____

15 Monday

Passage _______________

My Thoughts: _______________
____
____
____

My Application: _______________
____
____

16 Tuesday

Passage _______________

My Thoughts: _______________
____
____

My Application: _______________
____
____

17 Wednesday

Passage _______________

My Thoughts: _______________

____

____

____

My Application: _______________

____

____

18 Thursday

Passage _______________

My Thoughts: _______________

____

____

____

My Application: _______________

____

____

19 Friday

Passage _______________

My Thoughts: _______________

____

____

____

My Application: _______________

____

____

20 Saturday

Passage _______________

My Thoughts: _______________

____

____

My Application: _______________

____

____

JUNE

21 Sunday

Passage ________________________

My Thoughts: ____

____

____

____

My Application: ____

____

____

22 Monday

Passage ________________________

My Thoughts: ____

____

____

____

My Application: ____

____

____

23 Tuesday

Passage ________________________

My Thoughts: ____

____

____

____

My Application: ____

____

____

24 Wednesday

Passage ____________________

My Thoughts: ____

____

____

My Application: ____

____

____

25 Thursday

Passage ____________________

My Thoughts: ____

____

____

My Application: ____

____

____

26 Friday

Passage ____________________

My Thoughts: ____

____

____

My Application: ____

____

____

27 Saturday

Passage ____________________

My Thoughts: ____

____

____

My Application: ____

____

____

28 Sunday

Passage ___________________

My Thoughts: ___________________

____

____

____

My Application: ___________________

____

____

29 Monday

Passage ___________________

My Thoughts: ___________________

____

____

____

My Application: ___________________

____

____

30 Tuesday

Passage ___________________

My Thoughts: ___________________

____

____

My Application: ___________________

____

____

1 Wednesday

Passage _________________

My Thoughts: _____________________________________

____

____

____

My Application: __________________________________

____

____

2 Thursday

Passage _________________

My Thoughts: _____________________________________

____

____

____

My Application: __________________________________

____

____

3 Friday

Passage _________________

My Thoughts: _____________________________________

____

____

____

My Application: __________________________________

____

____

4 Saturday

Passage _________________

My Thoughts: _____________________________________

____

____

____

My Application: __________________________________

____

____

JULY

JULY 1992

S	M	T	W	T	F	S
			1	2	3	4
5	6	7	8	9	10	11
12	13	14	15	16	17	18
19	20	21	22	23	24	25
26	27	28	29	30	31	

5 Sunday

Passage ___________________

My Thoughts: ______________________________________

____

____

____

My Application: ______________________________________

____

____

6 Monday

Passage ___________________

My Thoughts: ______________________________________

____

____

____

My Application: ______________________________________

____

____

7 Tuesday

Passage ___________________

My Thoughts: ______________________________________

____

____

____

My Application: ______________________________________

____

____

8 Wednesday

Passage _______________________

My Thoughts: _______________________

____

____

My Application: _______________________

____

____

9 Thursday

Passage _______________________

My Thoughts: _______________________

____

____

My Application: _______________________

____

____

10 Friday

Passage _______________________

My Thoughts: _______________________

____

____

My Application: _______________________

____

____

11 Saturday

Passage _______________________

My Thoughts: _______________________

____

____

My Application: _______________________

____

____

JULY

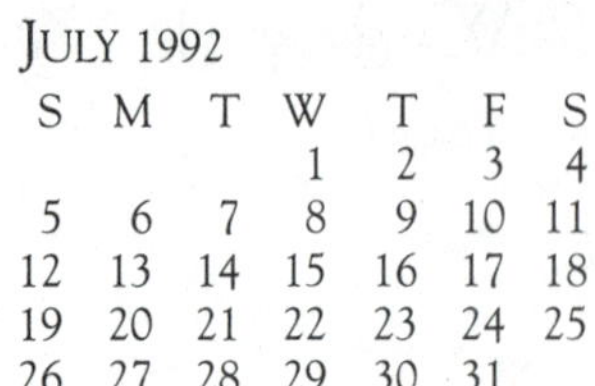

12 Sunday

Passage ________________________

My Thoughts: ________________________

____

____

____

My Application: ________________________

____

____

13 Monday

Passage ________________________

My Thoughts: ________________________

____

____

____

My Application: ________________________

____

____

14 Tuesday

Passage ________________________

My Thoughts: ________________________

____

____

____

My Application: ________________________

____

____

15 Wednesday

Passage _______________

My Thoughts: _______________

____

____

My Application: _______________

____

____

16 Thursday

Passage _______________

My Thoughts: _______________

____

____

____

My Application: _______________

____

____

17 Friday

Passage _______________

My Thoughts: _______________

____

____

____

My Application: _______________

____

____

18 Saturday

Passage _______________

My Thoughts: _______________

____

____

My Application: _______________

____

____

JULY

19 Sunday

Passage ______________________

My Thoughts: ____

____

____

____

My Application: ____

____

____

20 Monday

Passage ______________________

My Thoughts: ____

____

____

____

My Application: ____

____

____

21 Tuesday

Passage ______________________

My Thoughts: ____

____

____

____

My Application: ____

____

____

22 Wednesday

Passage _______________

My Thoughts: _______________

My Application: _______________

23 Thursday

Passage _______________

My Thoughts: _______________

My Application: _______________

24 Friday

Passage _______________

My Thoughts: _______________

My Application: _______________

25 Saturday

Passage _______________

My Thoughts: _______________

My Application: _______________

July

S	M	T	W	T	F	S
			1	2	3	4
5	6	7	8	9	10	11
12	13	14	15	16	17	18
19	20	21	22	23	24	25
26	27	28	29	30	31	

26 Sunday

Passage ________________________

My Thoughts: ________________________________

____

____

____

My Application: ______________________________

____

____

27 Monday

Passage ________________________

My Thoughts: ________________________________

____

____

____

My Application: ______________________________

____

____

28 Tuesday

Passage ________________________

My Thoughts: ________________________________

____

____

____

My Application: ______________________________

____

____

29 Wednesday

Passage _______________

My Thoughts: _______________

____

____

____

My Application: _______________

____

____

30 Thursday

Passage _______________

My Thoughts: _______________

____

____

____

My Application: _______________

____

____

31 Friday

Passage _______________

My Thoughts: _______________

____

____

____

My Application: _______________

____

____

1 Saturday

Passage _______________

My Thoughts: _______________

____

____

____

My Application: _______________

____

____

AUGUST

AUGUST 1992

S	M	T	W	T	F	S
						1
2	3	4	5	6	7	8
9	10	11	12	13	14	15
16	17	18	19	20	21	22
23	24	25	26	27	28	29
30	31					

2 Sunday

Passage _______________________

My Thoughts: _______________________

____

____

____

My Application: _____________________

____

____

3 Monday

Passage _______________________

My Thoughts: _______________________

____

____

____

My Application: _____________________

____

____

4 Tuesday

Passage _______________________

My Thoughts: _______________________

____

____

____

My Application: _____________________

____

____

5 Wednesday

Passage ______________________

My Thoughts: ______________________

____

____

____

My Application: ______________________

____

____

6 Thursday

Passage ______________________

My Thoughts: ______________________

____

____

____

My Application: ______________________

____

____

7 Friday

Passage ______________________

My Thoughts: ______________________

____

____

____

My Application: ______________________

____

____

8 Saturday

Passage ______________________

My Thoughts: ______________________

____

____

____

My Application: ______________________

____

____

AUGUST

<table>
<tr><td colspan="7">AUGUST 1992</td></tr>
<tr><td>S</td><td>M</td><td>T</td><td>W</td><td>T</td><td>F</td><td>S</td></tr>
<tr><td></td><td></td><td></td><td></td><td></td><td></td><td>1</td></tr>
<tr><td>2</td><td>3</td><td>4</td><td>5</td><td>6</td><td>7</td><td>8</td></tr>
<tr><td>9</td><td>10</td><td>11</td><td>12</td><td>13</td><td>14</td><td>15</td></tr>
<tr><td>16</td><td>17</td><td>18</td><td>19</td><td>20</td><td>21</td><td>22</td></tr>
<tr><td>23</td><td>24</td><td>25</td><td>26</td><td>27</td><td>28</td><td>29</td></tr>
<tr><td>30</td><td>31</td><td></td><td></td><td></td><td></td><td></td></tr>
</table>

9 Sunday

Passage ___________________

My Thoughts: ________________________________

____

____

____

My Application: ________________________________

____

____

10 Monday

Passage ___________________

My Thoughts: ________________________________

____

____

____

My Application: ________________________________

____

____

11 Tuesday

Passage ___________________

My Thoughts: ________________________________

____

____

My Application: ________________________________

____

____

12 Wednesday

Passage _______________

My Thoughts: _______________

____

____

____

My Application: _______________

____

____

13 Thursday

Passage _______________

My Thoughts: _______________

____

____

____

My Application: _______________

____

____

14 Friday

Passage _______________

My Thoughts: _______________

____

____

____

My Application: _______________

____

____

15 Saturday

Passage _______________

My Thoughts: _______________

____

____

____

My Application: _______________

____

____

AUGUST

<table>
<tr><td colspan="7">AUGUST 1992</td></tr>
<tr><td>S</td><td>M</td><td>T</td><td>W</td><td>T</td><td>F</td><td>S</td></tr>
<tr><td></td><td></td><td></td><td></td><td></td><td></td><td>1</td></tr>
<tr><td>2</td><td>3</td><td>4</td><td>5</td><td>6</td><td>7</td><td>8</td></tr>
<tr><td>9</td><td>10</td><td>11</td><td>12</td><td>13</td><td>14</td><td>15</td></tr>
<tr><td>16</td><td>17</td><td>18</td><td>19</td><td>20</td><td>21</td><td>22</td></tr>
<tr><td>23</td><td>24</td><td>25</td><td>26</td><td>27</td><td>28</td><td>29</td></tr>
<tr><td>30</td><td>31</td><td></td><td></td><td></td><td></td><td></td></tr>
</table>

16 Sunday

Passage _______________________

My Thoughts: _______________________________________

____

____

____

My Application: ___________________________________

____

____

17 Monday

Passage _______________________

My Thoughts: _______________________________________

____

____

____

My Application: ___________________________________

____

____

18 Tuesday

Passage _______________________

My Thoughts: _______________________________________

____

____

____

My Application: ___________________________________

____

____

19 Wednesday

Passage _______________________

My Thoughts: _______________________

____

____

____

My Application: _______________________

____

____

20 Thursday

Passage _______________________

My Thoughts: _______________________

____

____

____

My Application: _______________________

____

____

21 Friday

Passage _______________________

My Thoughts: _______________________

____

____

____

My Application: _______________________

____

____

22 Saturday

Passage _______________________

My Thoughts: _______________________

____

____

____

My Application: _______________________

____

____

AUGUST

AUGUST 1992

S	M	T	W	T	F	S
						1
2	3	4	5	6	7	8
9	10	11	12	13	14	15
16	17	18	19	20	21	22
23	24	25	26	27	28	29
30	31					

23 Sunday

Passage _______________________

My Thoughts: _______________________________________

____

____

____

My Application: ___________________________________

____

____

24 Monday

Passage _______________________

My Thoughts: _______________________________________

____

____

____

My Application: ___________________________________

____

____

25 Tuesday

Passage _______________________

My Thoughts: _______________________________________

____

____

My Application: ___________________________________

____

____

26 Wednesday

Passage _______________________

My Thoughts: _______________________

____

____

____

My Application: _______________________

____

____

27 Thursday

Passage _______________________

My Thoughts: _______________________

____

____

____

My Application: _______________________

____

____

28 Friday

Passage _______________________

My Thoughts: _______________________

____

____

____

My Application: _______________________

____

____

29 Saturday

Passage _______________________

My Thoughts: _______________________

____

____

____

My Application: _______________________

____

____

SEPTEMBER

S	M	T	W	T	F	S
		1	2	3	4	5
6	7	8	9	10	11	12
13	14	15	16	17	18	19
20	21	22	23	24	25	26
27	28	29	30			

30 Sunday

Passage _____________________

My Thoughts: _____________________

____

____

____

My Application: _____________________

____

____

31 Monday

Passage _____________________

My Thoughts: _____________________

____

____

____

My Application: _____________________

____

____

1 Tuesday

Passage _____________________

My Thoughts: _____________________

____

____

____

My Application: _____________________

____

____

2 Wednesday

Passage ___________________

My Thoughts: ___________________

____

____

My Application: ___________________

____

3 Thursday

Passage ___________________

My Thoughts: ___________________

____

____

My Application: ___________________

____

4 Friday

Passage ___________________

My Thoughts: ___________________

____

____

My Application: ___________________

____

5 Saturday

Passage ___________________

My Thoughts: ___________________

____

____

My Application: ___________________

____

SEPTEMBER

S	M	T	W	T	F	S
		1	2	3	4	5
6	7	8	9	10	11	12
13	14	15	16	17	18	19
20	21	22	23	24	25	26
27	28	29	30			

6 Sunday

Passage _______________________

My Thoughts: _______________________________________

____

____

____

My Application: ____________________________________

____

____

7 Monday

Passage _______________________

My Thoughts: _______________________________________

____

____

____

My Application: ____________________________________

____

____

8 Tuesday

Passage _______________________

My Thoughts: _______________________________________

____

____

My Application: ____________________________________

____

____

9 Wednesday

Passage ______________________

My Thoughts: _______________________

____

____

____

My Application: _____________________

____

____

10 Thursday

Passage ______________________

My Thoughts: _______________________

____

____

____

My Application: _____________________

____

____

11 Friday

Passage ______________________

My Thoughts: _______________________

____

____

____

My Application: _____________________

____

____

12 Saturday

Passage ______________________

My Thoughts: _______________________

____

____

____

My Application: _____________________

____

____

SEPTEMBER

13 Sunday

Passage _______________________

My Thoughts: _______________________

____

____

____

My Application: _______________________

____

____

14 Monday

Passage _______________________

My Thoughts: _______________________

____

____

____

My Application: _______________________

____

____

15 Tuesday

Passage _______________________

My Thoughts: _______________________

____

____

____

My Application: _______________________

____

____

16 Wednesday

Passage ___________________

My Thoughts: ___________________

____

____

____

My Application: ___________________

____

____

17 Thursday

Passage ___________________

My Thoughts: ___________________

____

____

____

My Application: ___________________

____

____

18 Friday

Passage ___________________

My Thoughts: ___________________

____

____

____

My Application: ___________________

____

____

19 Saturday

Passage ___________________

My Thoughts: ___________________

____

____

____

My Application: ___________________

____

____

SEPTEMBER

SEPTEMBER 1992

S	M	T	W	T	F	S
		1	2	3	4	5
6	7	8	9	10	11	12
13	14	15	16	17	18	19
20	21	22	23	24	25	26
27	28	29	30			

20 Sunday

Passage _______________________

My Thoughts: ____

____

____

____

My Application: ____

____

____

21 Monday

Passage _______________________

My Thoughts: ____

____

____

____

My Application: ____

____

____

22 Tuesday

Passage _______________________

My Thoughts: ____

____

____

My Application: ____

____

____

23 Wednesday

Passage _______________

My Thoughts: _______________

____

____

____

My Application: _______________

____

____

24 Thursday

Passage _______________

My Thoughts: _______________

____

____

____

My Application: _______________

____

____

25 Friday

Passage _______________

My Thoughts: _______________

____

____

____

My Application: _______________

____

____

26 Saturday

Passage _______________

My Thoughts: _______________

____

____

____

My Application: _______________

____

____

SEPTEMBER

S	M	T	W	T	F	S
		1	2	3	4	5
6	7	8	9	10	11	12
13	14	15	16	17	18	19
20	21	22	23	24	25	26
27	28	29	30			

27 Sunday

Passage ___________________

My Thoughts: ____

____

____

____

My Application: ____

____

____

28 Monday

Passage ___________________

My Thoughts: ____

____

____

____

My Application: ____

____

____

29 Tuesday

Passage ___________________

My Thoughts: ____

____

____

____

My Application: ____

____

____

30 Wednesday

Passage _______________

My Thoughts: _______________

____

____

____

My Application: _______________

____

____

1 Thursday

Passage _______________

My Thoughts: _______________

____

____

____

My Application: _______________

____

____

2 Friday

Passage _______________

My Thoughts: _______________

____

____

____

My Application: _______________

____

____

3 Saturday

Passage _______________

My Thoughts: _______________

____

____

My Application: _______________

____

____

OCTOBER

4 Sunday

Passage _______________________

My Thoughts: _______________________________________

____

____

____

My Application: ____________________________________

____

____

5 Monday

Passage _______________________

My Thoughts: _______________________________________

____

____

____

My Application: ____________________________________

____

____

6 Tuesday

Passage _______________________

My Thoughts: _______________________________________

____

____

____

My Application: ____________________________________

____

____

7 Wednesday

Passage _______________

My Thoughts: _______________

____

____

____

My Application: _______________

____

____

8 Thursday

Passage _______________

My Thoughts: _______________

____

____

____

My Application: _______________

____

____

9 Friday

Passage _______________

My Thoughts: _______________

____

____

____

My Application: _______________

____

____

10 Saturday

Passage _______________

My Thoughts: _______________

____

____

My Application: _______________

____

____

OCTOBER

11 Sunday

Passage _______________________

My Thoughts: _______________________________________

____

____

____

My Application: ___________________________________

____

____

12 Monday

Passage _______________________

My Thoughts: _______________________________________

____

____

____

My Application: ___________________________________

____

____

13 Tuesday

Passage _______________________

My Thoughts: _______________________________________

____

____

____

My Application: ___________________________________

____

____

14 Wednesday

Passage ___________________

My Thoughts: ____

____

____

My Application: _______________________________________

____

____

15 Thursday

Passage ___________________

My Thoughts: ____

____

____

My Application: _______________________________________

____

____

16 Friday

Passage ___________________

My Thoughts: ____

____

____

My Application: _______________________________________

____

____

17 Saturday

Passage ___________________

My Thoughts: ____

____

____

My Application: _______________________________________

____

____

OCTOBER

S	M	T	W	T	F	S
				1	2	3
4	5	6	7	8	9	10
11	12	13	14	15	16	17
18	19	20	21	22	23	24
25	26	27	28	29	30	31

18 Sunday

Passage ______________________

My Thoughts: ____

____

____

____

My Application: ______________________________________

____

____

19 Monday

Passage ______________________

My Thoughts: ____

____

____

____

My Application: ______________________________________

____

____

20 Tuesday

Passage ______________________

My Thoughts: ____

____

____

My Application: ______________________________________

____

____

21 Wednesday

Passage _______________________

My Thoughts: _______________________

____

____

____

My Application: _______________________

____

____

22 Thursday

Passage _______________________

My Thoughts: _______________________

____

____

____

My Application: _______________________

____

____

23 Friday

Passage _______________________

My Thoughts: _______________________

____

____

____

My Application: _______________________

____

____

24 Saturday

Passage _______________________

My Thoughts: _______________________

____

____

____

My Application: _______________________

____

____

OCTOBER

OCTOBER 1992

S	M	T	W	T	F	S
				1	2	3
4	5	6	7	8	9	10
11	12	13	14	15	16	17
18	19	20	21	22	23	24
25	26	27	28	29	30	31

25 Sunday

Passage _______________

My Thoughts: _______________________________

My Application: _____________________________

26 Monday

Passage _______________

My Thoughts: _______________________________

My Application: _____________________________

27 Tuesday

Passage _______________

My Thoughts: _______________________________

My Application: _____________________________

28 Wednesday

Passage ______________________

My Thoughts: ______________________

____

____

____

My Application: ______________________

____

____

29 Thursday

Passage ______________________

My Thoughts: ______________________

____

____

____

My Application: ______________________

____

____

30 Friday

Passage ______________________

My Thoughts: ______________________

____

____

____

My Application: ______________________

____

____

31 Saturday

Passage ______________________

My Thoughts: ______________________

____

____

____

My Application: ______________________

____

____

November

November 1992

S	M	T	W	T	F	S
1	2	3	4	5	6	7
8	9	10	11	12	13	14
15	16	17	18	19	20	21
22	23	24	25	26	27	28
29	30					

1 Sunday

Passage _______________

My Thoughts: _____________________________________

My Application: __________________________________

2 Monday

Passage _______________

My Thoughts: _____________________________________

My Application: __________________________________

3 Tuesday

Passage _______________

My Thoughts: _____________________________________

My Application: __________________________________

4 Wednesday

Passage ______________________

My Thoughts: _________________________________

____

____

____

My Application: ______________________________

____

____

5 Thursday

Passage ______________________

My Thoughts: _________________________________

____

____

____

My Application: ______________________________

____

____

6 Friday

Passage ______________________

My Thoughts: _________________________________

____

____

____

My Application: ______________________________

____

____

7 Saturday

Passage ______________________

My Thoughts: _________________________________

____

____

My Application: ______________________________

____

____

November

8 Sunday

Passage _______________

My Thoughts: _______________

My Application: _______________

9 Monday

Passage _______________

My Thoughts: _______________

My Application: _______________

10 Tuesday

Passage _______________

My Thoughts: _______________

My Application: _______________

11 Wednesday

Passage ___________________

My Thoughts: ___________________

____

____

My Application: ___________________

____

12 Thursday

Passage ___________________

My Thoughts: ___________________

____

____

My Application: ___________________

____

13 Friday

Passage ___________________

My Thoughts: ___________________

____

____

My Application: ___________________

____

14 Saturday

Passage ___________________

My Thoughts: ___________________

____

____

My Application: ___________________

____

NOVEMBER

15 Sunday

Passage ______________________

My Thoughts: ______________________

____

____

____

My Application: ______________________

____

____

16 Monday

Passage ______________________

My Thoughts: ______________________

____

____

My Application: ______________________

____

____

17 Tuesday

Passage ______________________

My Thoughts: ______________________

____

____

My Application: ______________________

____

____

18 Wednesday

Passage _______________________

My Thoughts: _______________________

____

____

____

My Application: _______________________

____

____

19 Thursday

Passage _______________________

My Thoughts: _______________________

____

____

____

My Application: _______________________

____

____

20 Friday

Passage _______________________

My Thoughts: _______________________

____

____

____

My Application: _______________________

____

____

21 Saturday

Passage _______________________

My Thoughts: _______________________

____

____

____

My Application: _______________________

____

____

NOVEMBER

22 Sunday

Passage _______________

My Thoughts: ____

____

____

____

My Application: ____

____

____

23 Monday

Passage _______________

My Thoughts: ____

____

____

____

My Application: ____

____

____

24 Tuesday

Passage _______________

My Thoughts: ____

____

____

____

My Application: ____

____

____

25 Wednesday

Passage ___________________

My Thoughts: ___________________________________

____

____

____

My Application: ___________________________________

____

____

26 Thursday

Passage ___________________

My Thoughts: ___________________________________

____

____

____

My Application: ___________________________________

____

____

27 Friday

Passage ___________________

My Thoughts: ___________________________________

____

____

____

My Application: ___________________________________

____

____

28 Saturday

Passage ___________________

My Thoughts: ___________________________________

____

____

My Application: ___________________________________

____

____

December

29 Sunday

Passage _______________

My Thoughts: _______________

____

My Application: _______________

30 Monday

Passage _______________

My Thoughts: _______________

____

My Application: _______________

1 Tuesday

Passage _______________

My Thoughts: _______________

____

My Application: _______________

2 Wednesday

Passage _______________

My Thoughts: _______________________________________

____

____

____

My Application: ___________________________________

____

____

3 Thursday

Passage _______________

My Thoughts: _______________________________________

____

____

____

My Application: ___________________________________

____

____

4 Friday

Passage _______________

My Thoughts: _______________________________________

____

____

____

My Application: ___________________________________

____

____

5 Saturday

Passage _______________

My Thoughts: _______________________________________

____

____

____

My Application: ___________________________________

____

____

DECEMBER

S	M	T	W	T	F	S
		1	2	3	4	5
6	7	8	9	10	11	12
13	14	15	16	17	18	19
20	21	22	23	24	25	26
27	28	29	30	31		

6 Sunday

Passage _______________________

My Thoughts: ____

____

____

____

My Application: ____

____

____

7 Monday

Passage _______________________

My Thoughts: ____

____

____

____

My Application: ____

____

____

8 Tuesday

Passage _______________________

My Thoughts: ____

____

____

____

My Application: ____

____

____

9 Wednesday

Passage _______________

My Thoughts: _______________

____

____

____

My Application: _______________

____

____

10 Thursday

Passage _______________

My Thoughts: _______________

____

____

____

My Application: _______________

____

____

11 Friday

Passage _______________

My Thoughts: _______________

____

____

____

My Application: _______________

____

____

12 Saturday

Passage _______________

My Thoughts: _______________

____

____

____

My Application: _______________

____

____

DECEMBER

13 Sunday

Passage ___________________

My Thoughts: _______________________________________

____

____

____

My Application: ___________________________________

____

____

14 Monday

Passage ___________________

My Thoughts: _______________________________________

____

____

____

My Application: ___________________________________

____

____

15 Tuesday

Passage ___________________

My Thoughts: _______________________________________

____

____

____

My Application: ___________________________________

____

____

16 Wednesday

Passage ___________________

My Thoughts: ___________________
____
____
____

My Application: ___________________
____
____

17 Thursday

Passage ___________________

My Thoughts: ___________________
____
____
____

My Application: ___________________
____
____

18 Friday

Passage ___________________

My Thoughts: ___________________
____
____
____

My Application: ___________________
____
____

19 Saturday

Passage ___________________

My Thoughts: ___________________
____
____
____

My Application: ___________________
____
____

DECEMBER

20 Sunday

Passage _______________________

My Thoughts: _______________________

____

____

____

My Application: _______________________

____

____

21 Monday

Passage _______________________

My Thoughts: _______________________

____

____

____

My Application: _______________________

____

____

22 Tuesday

Passage _______________________

My Thoughts: _______________________

____

____

____

My Application: _______________________

____

____

23 Wednesday

Passage _______________________

My Thoughts: _______________________

____

____

____

My Application: _______________________

____

____

24 Thursday

Passage _______________________

My Thoughts: _______________________

____

____

____

My Application: _______________________

____

____

25 Friday

Passage _______________________

My Thoughts: _______________________

____

____

____

My Application: _______________________

____

____

26 Saturday

Passage _______________________

My Thoughts: _______________________

____

____

____

My Application: _______________________

____

____

December

S	M	T	W	T	F	S
		1	2	3	4	5
6	7	8	9	10	11	12
13	14	15	16	17	18	19
20	21	22	23	24	25	26
27	28	29	30	31		

27 Sunday

Passage _______________

My Thoughts: _______________________________

____

____

____

My Application: ____________________________

____

____

28 Monday

Passage _______________

My Thoughts: _______________________________

____

____

____

My Application: ____________________________

____

____

29 Tuesday

Passage _______________

My Thoughts: _______________________________

____

____

____

My Application: ____________________________

____

____

30 Wednesday

Passage ______________________

My Thoughts: ________________________________

____

____

____

My Application: ____________________________

____

____

31 Thursday

Passage ______________________

My Thoughts: ________________________________

____

____

____

My Application: ____________________________

____

____

1 Friday

Passage ______________________

My Thoughts: ________________________________

____

____

____

My Application: ____________________________

____

____

2 Saturday

Passage ______________________

My Thoughts: ________________________________

____

____

____

My Application: ____________________________

____

____

One-Year Bible Survey

1st Quarter: Genesis–2 Samuel
2nd Quarter: 1 Kings–Malachi
3rd Quarter: Matthew–Acts
4th Quarter: Romans–Revelation

1st Quarter:
Genesis–2 Samuel

WEEK 1

(Genesis) God's Early Dealings With Mankind

That the world is not what it should be is obvious to Christian and non-Christian alike. But how did things get to be so bad? And is there any hope that they will ever get better? The opening chapters of Genesis answer the first question, and provide the beginnings of an answer to the second question.

☐ **Gen. 1:1–25 God creates the universe out of nothing.**
What is present, besides God, at the creation? With what does God create the universe? Does he like what he has created?

☐ **1:26–2:25 God creates mankind "in his own image."**
Does Genesis say anything about *why* God created mankind? What "assignments" does God give mankind? Why does God place one restriction on man's freedom?

☐ **3:1–24 The first man and woman rebel against God.**
What causes Adam and Eve to disobey God? What are the immediate results of their sin? What would be the long-range results? (See 2:17.) What is the significance of verse 15?

☐ **4:1–16 Sin is passed on to the second generation of mankind.**
How does Romans 5:12–14 explain what happens in chapter 4? How does God show mercy to Cain?

☐ **6:1–7:5 Wickedness fills the earth; God says he'll destroy it.**
How does 6:5 describe the wickedness of Noah's time? How does it compare to our world today? What sort of person must Noah have been to have "found favor" in God's eyes?

☐ **7:6–8:22 One righteous family is allowed to survive.**
What must life have been like for Noah and his family while they were building the ark? While they were *in* the ark?

☐ **9:1–27 Yet sin is still present, even in this righteous family.**
What promise does God make to mankind? Did the flood totally wash away man's sinful nature?

WEEK 2

(Genesis) God Chooses One Nation

By now it is obvious that sin has brought continual suffering and death to mankind and has destroyed his fellowship with God. But God is already working to save his people and give them eternal life. In these chapters we see him setting apart a nation to be his special means of bringing salvation.

☐ **Gen. 11:1–12:5 Wickedness continues; God chooses Abram.** Why was building the Tower of Babel wrong? How does God's promise to Abram in 12:2 answer the felt needs of the Babel builders (11:4).

☐ **15:1–21; 17:1–8 God makes a promise to Abram.** Why does Abram doubt God's promise? How does God reassure him? How does his new name help confirm God's promise?

☐ **19:1–29 Sodom and Gomorrah are destroyed for their sin.** How does Sodom and Gomorrah's wickedness compare with our own day? Why does God tell Lot and his family not to look back as they flee?

☐ **21:1–7; 22:1–18 Abraham's faith is put to the test.** Why might Abraham have a hard time understanding God's command (22:2) in light of his earlier promise (12:2)? What must he have been thinking as he set out to sacrifice his son? (See Hebrews 11:17–19.)

☐ **25:19–34; 27:1–40 Jacob steals his brother's birthright.** We now read about Abraham's grandson, Jacob. What do these events reveal about Jacob's character? What do they reveal about God's grace?

☐ **27:41–28:22 Jacob inherits God's promise to Abraham.** What does Jacob have to do as the result of his treachery? How is God's grace displayed once again? How well does Jacob understand God's grace?

☐ **32:1–32 God changes Jacob's name to Israel.** Why is Jacob afraid of a reunion with Esau? Compare Jacob's attitude in 9–12 with 28:16–22. How did the events of 22–29 affect him?

WEEK 3

(Genesis) Joseph Saves Israel From Famine

Israel has twelve sons and one daughter. Although the kings of Israel and the promised Messiah will descend from his son Judah, another of his sons, Joseph, now becomes the focus of the story. As we get to know this outstanding young man, we'll understand why.

☐ **Gen. 37:1–28 Joseph's brothers sell him as a slave.**
Why are Joseph's brothers jealous of him? How does each person involved react to the events of this chapter?

☐ **39:1–23 Joseph is honored, imprisoned, and honored again.**
What causes Joseph's first "success" in Egypt (3–4)? In what sense is his encounter with Potiphar's wife also a success? How does he succeed in prison?

☐ **41:1–57 Joseph is put in charge of Egypt.**
Why is Joseph put in charge of Egypt? How does he do in this new job?

☐ **42:1–38 His brothers come to Egypt in search of food.**
Was Joseph justified in demanding to see Benjamin (15)? Did he have valid reasons to fear for his safety? (See 37:3, then 35:24.) What secret guilt controls the brothers' actions (21)? How does Joseph show mercy?

☐ **43:1–34 They return a second time, bringing Benjamin.**
Describe the emotions of the various people in this chapter. How did Judah play the key role (8–10).

☐ **44:1–34 Joseph tests his brothers further.**
Once again, how does Judah play a key role (44:16–34)? Compare this to his role in 37:26–27. Note how guilt over the brothers' past sin against Joseph still haunts them (16).

☐ **45:1–28; 50:15–21 Joseph shows mercy to his brothers.**
Is it hard for Joseph to forgive his brothers, or did he want to all along? (See 42:24; 43:30; 45:1–2.) Note in chapter 50 that, many years later, the brothers still feel guilty, and Joseph is still willing to forgive!

WEEK 4

(Exodus) Israel Is Saved From Bondage in Egypt

Israel and his family move to Egypt. Years pass, their numbers multiply greatly, and the Egyptians begin to persecute them. But God does not forget his chosen people. He promises to rescue them from Egypt and lead them to a land of their own.

☐ **Ex. 1:1–2:25 Israel is oppressed; a deliverer is born.**
Why did the Egyptians persecute the Israelites? How does Moses happen to grow up in Pharaoh's palace? Does Moses identify more with the Egyptians he grew up with, or with his own oppressed people?

☐ **3:1–4:31 God calls Moses.**
What are God's plans for Israel? For Moses? How does Numbers 12:3 help explain Moses' response to God's call (3:11; 4:1, 10)? How does God try to build up Moses' confidence?

☐ **5:1–6:12 The first encounter with Pharaoh.**
What is the result of Moses and Aaron's first appearance before Pharaoh? How does God reassure them? What does he once again promise them?

☐ **6:28–7:24 Moses demonstrates God's power to Pharaoh.**
What is Pharaoh's response to the plagues in this and the following chapters (see 7:13, 22; 8:15, 19; 9:7, 12, etc.)?

☐ **11:1–12:42 Egypt's firstborn die; Pharaoh lets Israel go.**
How does Pharaoh respond to this last terrible plague? Why does God give the Israelites such specific instructions for their final night in Egypt? How is Christ "our passover lamb" (1 Cor. 5:7)?

☐ **13:17–14:31 The Israelites cross the Red Sea.**
What does 14:5–8 suggest about Pharaoh's sorrow for his own son's death? What does 14:10–12 suggest about the Israelites' appreciation for what God is doing for them? How do they respond to the miracle at the Red Sea?

☐ **15:22–17:7 The first days in the wilderness.**
In what ways does the manna and quail provide perfectly for Israel's needs? What is their attitude toward the Lord's provision?

WEEK 5

(Exodus) God Gives Israel a Law to Live By

God has promised that the land of Canaan, where Abraham, Isaac, and Jacob had "lived as aliens" (6:4) would be given to Israel. Now, as he leads them to their new homeland, he gives them a law by which to govern themselves.

☐ **Ex. 19:1–25 Israel prepares to receive the Law.**
Why did God say he was giving the Law to Israel (4–6)? How did Moses prepare the people to receive the Law?

☐ **20:1–21 The Ten Commandments.**
Think about how each of these commandments could help Israel become a strong nation. How many of these commandments does our society uphold today? How many of them do *Christians* uphold today?

☐ **21:12–36 Laws concerning personal injuries.**
We'll now look at a brief sampling of the laws given at Sinai. How are these very specific personal injury laws examples of God's grace.

☐ **22:1–31 Laws concerning personal property.**
How would the principle of restitution promote a stable society? Could it work today? What groups are given special protection in verses 21–27?

☐ **23:1–9 Laws concerning justice.**
What is the overriding principle in seeing that the poor receive justice (3, 6)? What are some other principles of justice in these verses?

☐ **23:20–33 The importance of being a holy nation.**
Why does God emphasize so much the need for his people to remain separate from the Canaanites?

☐ **32:1–35 The golden calf.**
How do the events of this chapter demonstrate the importance of what we just heard God say in 23:20–33?

WEEK 6

(Numbers) Israel Journeys Toward Canaan

Leviticus and the first nine chapters of Numbers complete the initial giving of the Law at Mount Sinai. The rest of Numbers tells of the Israelites' journey toward the Promised Land. It is a story of God's faithfulness in spite of Israel's continual acts of rebellion, including two events with especially disastrous consequences.

☐ **Num. 10:11–11:35 Israel complains and is punished.**
What is the predominant attitude among the Israelites in chapter 11? What effect does this have on Moses? What does God do about the situation?

☐ **12:1–16 Miriam and Aaron oppose Moses.**
How do the attitudes of Miriam and Aaron compare with that of Moses?

☐ **13:1–33 Spying out the Promised Land.**
How must the Israelites have felt as they stood at the very door of their new homeland? How do most of the spies respond to what they see on the spy expedition?

☐ **14:1–38 Israel loses faith and is turned back.**
How do the Israelites respond to the reports of the spies? What is the disastrous result of their negative attitude?

☐ **16:1–35 Moses deals with another rebellion.**
What was the basic complaint against Moses (3)? What was Moses' attitude toward the rebels? Why was the punishment so severe?

☐ **17:1–13 The budding of Aaron's rod.**
Why, in light of the events of chapter 16, is the miraculous sign in chapter 17 necessary?

☐ **20:1–12 Moses strikes the rock and is judged by God.**
What thoughts must have been going through Moses' mind in this passage? What is his sin, and his punishment?

WEEK 7

(Deuteronomy) The Final Teachings of Moses

The forty years of wilderness wandering have been completed and Israel stands, once again, at the doorstep of the Promised Land. Deuteronomy consists mainly of the final exhortations Moses gives his people—reminding them of all that God has done, and urging them to rededicate themselves as they enter the land.

☐ **Deut. 6:1–25 Teach your children the Law.**
Why, according to Moses, did God give the Law to Israel? Why does Moses stress teaching the Law to children? How well do Christians today follow this practice?

☐ **7:1–26 Keep yourselves pure.**
Why are the nations of Canaan to be destroyed? Why, according to verses 7–8, did God choose Israel? How will Israel be rewarded for obedience?

☐ **8:1-20 Do not forget your wilderness wanderings.**
What lessons should Israel learn from forty years in the wilderness? What will happen if they forget those lessons (10–20)?

☐ **11:1–32 Love and obey God.**
What does Moses remind the people of in verses 1–7? What are they promised if they love and obey God?

☐ **13:1–18 Do not worship any other gods.**
From what sources might Israel be tempted to follow other gods? Do we experience temptation from these same sources today?

☐ **28:1–68 Blessings for obedience; curses for disobedience.**
Why are the curses for disobedience (15–68) so much more lengthy and graphic than the blessings for obedience (1–14)?

☐ **30:11–20 The choice is yours.**
What two options does Moses ask Israel to choose between? Should it be a difficult choice to make?

WEEK 8

(Joshua) The Conquest of Canaan

With Moses dead, Joshua takes over leadership of Israel as they enter and conquer the Promised Land. God allows Israel to conquer Canaan as a judgment upon Canaan's sins. But Israel must fight each battle courageously in order to claim as theirs the land they once were afraid to enter.

☐ **Josh. 1:1–18 God prepares Joshua for leadership.**
What command does God twice give Joshua (6–9)? Note that this seems to have become Israel's "fight song" by verse 18.

☐ **2:1–24 Spying out Jericho.**
How did the people of Jericho view the Israelites (8–13)? Do you think any of the Israelites still viewed themselves as grasshoppers (Num. 13:33)?

☐ **3:1–17 Crossing the Jordan.**
How does God "exalt" Joshua (7) in the eyes of Israel? What previous leader of Israel was exalted in this way? Why did God do this?

☐ **4:1–24 The memorial in the river.**
What two events does the memorial in the Jordan help the people remember?

☐ **5:1–6:27 Jericho is taken.**
Why is Jericho "tightly shut up" (6:1)? (See 5:1.) Why does God prescribe such a strange method for conquering Jericho? How is Rahab rewarded for her courage? (See Matt. 1:5.)

☐ **10:1–15 The day the sun stood still.**
What do the events of this chapter say about Joshua's faith? About God's grace?

☐ **24:1–33 Joshua's farewell message.**
How are Joshua's farewell words similar to those of Moses? (Compare 14–15 with Deut. 30:19–20.) How do the people respond to Joshua's challenge?

WEEK 9

(Judges) Israel's Early Days in Canaan

The book of Judges spans several hundred years following the conquest of Canaan. Here we find Israel going through an endless cycle of rebellion against God, followed by military defeat, followed by repentance, followed by deliverance by a military leader, or "judge." Although God is always faithful to save them, Israel never quite learns that sin brings judgment.

☐ **Judg. 1:1–2:23 The "younger generation" turns against God.**
What do you think will be the outcome of the failures recorded in 1:27–36? (See 2:1–3.) What connection do you see between 2:10 and Deut. 6:6–9?

☐ **3:7–4:24 The cycle: Sin, judgment, repentance, deliverance.**
Notice the four-part cycle of events in 3:7–9, 11, repeated in 12, 15, 30, and beginning again in 4:1–4. How would you describe Deborah's leadership qualities as she delivers Israel?

☐ **6:1–40 God calls Gideon to save Israel.**
How are the events of 6:1–10 part of a familiar pattern? How is Gideon's response to God's call (11–40) similar to the way Moses responded (Ex. 3:1–4:17)?

☐ **7:1–25 Gideon defeats the Midianites.**
How is the battle plan God prescribes for Gideon similar to what happened at Jericho? Why do you think God used such unusual methods?

☐ **13:1–14:20 The birth and early life of Samson.**
What familiar events (13:1) set the stage for Samson's career? While Samson is noted mainly for his exploits of strength, what do verses 13:25 and 14:19 say about him?

☐ **15:1–20 Further exploits of Samson.**
How does God use Samson's very human motives for his own purposes? What does verse 20 tell us about Samson's *inner* strength?

☐ **16:1–31 Samson's last day.**
God used Samson, in many ways a very worldly man, to begin (13:5) delivering Israel from the Philistines. What does that say about God's sovereignty and grace?

WEEK 10

(Judges, Ruth) The Worst Times; The Best People

As the book of Judges draws to a close, things seem to become progressively worse. We read stories of unbelievable social chaos and brutality. But Ruth also lived in that time period; her story shows that God's people can pursue lives of dignity and grace even in the most ungodly surroundings.

☐ **Judg. 19:1–30 Israel at the depths of depravity.**
How does the depravity described in 22–30 compare to the wickedness of Sodom? How does the nation react? (See 29–30; see also Hosea 9:9—they were still talking about it centuries later!)

☐ **20:1–48 The Benjamites fail to prosecute the offenders.**
Because those in authority refused to pursue justice, a local sin becomes a national disaster.

☐ **21:1–25 An ungodly solution for an ungodly situation.**
How does verse 25 help explain the events of these last three chapters of Judges? Of the entire book?

☐ **Ruth 1:1–22 Ruth's love for her Israelite mother-in-law.**
Why is Ruth's loyalty to Naomi commendable in light of 11–13? Why is the love between Ruth and Naomi remarkable in light of Judg. 3:12–30?

☐ **2:1–23 Ruth and Naomi find help in Israel.**
For widows in those days, the only hope for security was the generosity of relatives. How does this explain the events of chapter 2? How was Ruth's kindness to Naomi repaid?

☐ **3:1–18 A marriage is proposed.**
According to the custom of the day, it was Boaz's duty to either find a husband for Ruth or marry her himself. How does this explain the events of chapter 3?

☐ **4:1–22 Boaz and Ruth are married.**
Why are the integrity, loyalty, and kindness of Naomi, Ruth, and Boaz remarkable in light of Judg. 21:25? What great blessing to the whole world came from this marriage?

WEEK 11

(1 Samuel) Samuel, Saul, and David

The book of 1 Samuel opens with the story of Samuel, Israel's last judge and a great religious leader as well. The people of Israel ask for a king, and Saul is chosen. Then, as Saul falls into sin and brings down God's judgment, the focus of the story shifts to a young shepherd boy who is destined to become Israel's second and greatest king.

☐ **1 Sam. 8:1–22 Israel asks for a king.**
Why did Israel want a king (5, 20)? How did this go against God's special plan for Israel (see Lev. 20:26)? What dangers did Samuel warn them of?

☐ **9:1–27 Saul is chosen to be king.**
From the description of Saul in verse 2, is he the kind of king Israel wanted (8:20)? How does Saul feel about being made king?

☐ **10:1–27 Samuel anoints Saul.**
How does Samuel feel about the coronation of the new king (19, 24)? How do the people feel (24–27)? What does verse 22 say about Saul?

☐ **13:1–14 Samuel rebukes Saul.**
For what sin does Samuel rebuke Saul (compare verse 9 with Num. 18:5–7)? How does he disobey the "job description" of a king (Deut. 17:14–20)? What kind of man will replace Saul (14)?

☐ **15:1–26 The Lord rejects Saul.**
What is God's command to Saul (3)? How well does Saul follow the command? What is the result?

☐ **16:1–23 Samuel anoints David as king.**
How is the new king to be different than Saul? What two things help prepare David to be king (13, 21)?

☐ **17:1–58 David and Goliath.**
How do the events of this chapter pave the way for David becoming king?

WEEK 12

(1, 2 Samuel) David Becomes King

As King Saul sinks deeper into depravity, ultimately taking his own life, David proves himself a man worthy to be Israel's next king. As 2 Samuel opens, David is officially named Saul's successor. But even in his hour of triumph he sincerely mourns the loss of Saul.

☐ **1 Sam. 18:1–30 Saul becomes jealous of David.**
What events originally lead to Saul's jealousy of David? What does his increasing jealousy tell us about Saul?

☐ **19:1–24 Saul tries to kill David.**
Why is Saul so eager to kill David? What people help David escape?

☐ **24:1–22 David spares Saul's life.**
What do the events of this chapter say about David's respect for Saul? About his reverence for God?

☐ **28:1–31:13 Saul kills himself.**
How do the events of chapter 28 represent the depths of moral depravity? Does Saul's suicide seem like a fitting end for his life?

☐ **2 Sam. 1:1–27 David's sorrow over Saul.**
What do David's actions in 1–16 say about his respect for the office of king? What does his expression of sorrow for Saul say about his character? (See 1 Sam. 13:14.)

☐ **5:1–25 David is officially made king.**
What historic victory does David win as he becomes king? How does God then show David that *he* is still the one who gives victory?

☐ **7:1–8:18 God's promise to David.**
What promise, important to all of human history, does God make to David? What long-time enemy does David finally defeat?

WEEK 13

(2 Samuel) David: Saint and Sinner

These chapters show King David at his best and worst—as a man after God's own heart, and a man who will commit murder to have the woman with whom he has already committed adultery. As chapter 9 opens, we see him showing kindness to the son of Jonathan, King Saul's son and David's best friend (see 1 Sam. 18–20), who had died the same day Saul died.

☐ **2 Sam. 9:1–13 David's generosity to Mephibosheth.**
Besides his love for Jonathan, why did David show kindness to Mephibosheth? Why was Mephibosheth in need of such help?

☐ **11:1–27 David and Bathsheba.**
What circumstances originally led to David's sin? How did David compound his initial wrongdoing?

☐ **12:1–25 Nathan convicts David of his sin.**
What does Nathan say will be the result of David's sin (8–12)? David wrote Psalm 51 during this time. What does it say about the sincerity of David's repentance?

☐ **15:1–37 David's son Absalom rebels against him.**
Chapters 13 and 14 tell of the turmoil that came to David's family as a result of his sin. How is this brought to a climax in chapter 15?

☐ **16:1–23 Absalom seizes the throne.**
How does Absalom fulfill the prophecy of Nathan (12:8–12)? How does this compare to the moral degradation of Sodom? Of our own day?

☐ **17:1–29 Absalom follows the wrong advice.**
How does Absalom's pride get him into trouble?

☐ **18:1–33 The death of Absalom.**
Is Absalom's death "poetic justice"? What godly quality do we see in David's response? (Compare this to 1:1–27.)

2nd Quarter:
1 Kings–Malachi

WEEK 1

(1 Kings) Israel in Glory and Decline

1 and 2 Kings together cover about 350 years, from the death of King David to the time when both the northern and southern kingdoms have been conquered and taken into exile. In 1 Kings we see how immorality begins to destroy Israel. (The books in this quarter's survey will appear in approximate historical order, rather than canonical order.)

☐ **1 Kings 1:28–2:12 Solomon becomes king.**
What are the various responses to news of Solomon's coronation? What kind of advice does David give Solomon?

☐ **3:1–28; 4:20–34 Solomon asks for wisdom.**
Why does Solomon ask for wisdom? What does God give him in addition to wisdom? How is his wisdom demonstrated in chapter 3?

☐ **5:1–6:38 Solomon builds the temple.**
How is the promise of 2 Sam. 7:1–16 partially fulfilled here? Why was David not allowed to build the temple? (See 5:3; 1 Chron. 28:2–3).

☐ **10:1–11:43 Solomon's wives lead him astray.**
Why are the things reported in chapter 11 so tragic, in light of what we read about Solomon in chapter 10? How does Deut. 17:14-20 relate to this passage?

☐ **12:1–24 The kingdom is divided.**
How do the tragic events of this chapter compare to the fate of David's family after his sin with Bathsheba (2 Sam. 15:1–37)?

☐ **16:29–19:21 Ahab and Elijah.**
Describe the "moral warfare" between Ahab and Elijah. In what ways does God make his power and presence known during these dark days?

☐ **21:1–29 Ahab and Naboth.**
How does this chapter show the utter wickedness of King Ahab? Who does Elijah say will suffer for Ahab's sins?

WEEK 2

(2 Kings) The Two Kingdoms Are Conquered

During the 250 years covered by 2 Kings, the two kingdoms continue to fall into paganism and immorality, God keeps on sending prophets to warn them of judgment and, ultimately, first Israel and then Judah are conquered and taken into exile.

☐ **2 Kings 2:1–25 Elisha succeeds Elijah.**
How must Elisha have felt after witnessing the glorious climax of his predecessor's ministry? How is his own ministry confirmed?

☐ **4:1–5:27 The ministry of Elisha.**
How does Elisha's ministry show God's faithfulness to those who follow him during times of moral depravity?

☐ **10:1–35 The curse on Ahab's family is fulfilled.**
How is the prophecy of 1 Kings 21:21 fulfilled here? Why is Jehu, though zealous for God, a failure in the end?

☐ **12:1–21 Joash repairs the temple.**
Why did Joash, although he restored the temple, fail to save Judah from its slide toward destruction?

☐ **17:7–23 The northern kingdom of Israel goes into captivity.**
Verses 7–9 state clearly the reason for Israel's tragic fate. What is it?

☐ **18:1–19:37 Hezekiah, Sennacherib, and Isaiah.**
How does Hezekiah "rate" among the kings (18:5)? Why? How close does Judah come to destruction at this time (13)? What is Hezekiah's response? What does Isaiah predict? How is Judah saved?

☐ **23:36–25:30 Jerusalem falls; Judah goes into captivity.**
A hundred years have passed since God saved Judah in Hezekiah's day. How do Judah's last three kings help bring about its fall? Does there seem to be any hope that Israel will survive as a nation?

WEEK 3

(Psalms) Israel's Book of Worship

Psalms is Israel's book of worship. In its poetry we find expressed every emotion known to mankind. The message of the Psalms is two-fold: We should not be afraid to lay all our feelings, both negative and positive, at God's throne of grace; but in the midst of those problems, our primary focus should be on his glory and majesty.

☐ **Ps. 8:1–9 "How majestic is your name!"**
What about God amazes David? In what way is mankind small? In what way is he great?

☐ **10:1–18 "Do not forget the helpless."**
How are wicked people portrayed in this psalm? Does this seem to be true of wicked people today? What is the only help of their victims?

☐ **22:1–31 "Why have you forsaken me?"**
Would this be good reading for someone struggling with depression? Once David is over his depression, what does he promise to do (22–31)? Where does verse 1 reappear in Scripture?

☐ **24:1–10 "The earth is the Lord's."**
Why should we worship God, according to this psalm? What preparations should we make before we worship him?

☐ **33:1–22 Lord of creation, Lord of his people.**
How did God create the world? What should be our response to that fact? Would a citizen of Israel have felt proud or ashamed as he read 12–19?

☐ **37:1–40 Do not envy the wicked.**
How does David contrast the wicked and the righteous? How is the word *wait* a key to understanding this psalm? What are some other key words?

☐ **39:1–13 "Show me the number of my days."**
Why is the activity David describes in verse 6 so useless in the end? How does David say we can overcome this sense of life's futility?

WEEK 4

(Psalms) How to Worship; How to Live

In Colossians 3:16 Paul speaks of the mutual edification that can come from worship as well as from Bible study. As we read the Psalms, we learn not just how to worship, but how to live.

☐ **Ps. 42:1–11 "My soul thirsts for God."**
What causes the psalmist to thirst for God? Why do "down times" often turn our thoughts to spiritual things?

☐ **51:1–19 "Have mercy on me, O God."**
What phrases in this psalm show that David was truly sorry for his sin with Bathsheba? How does verse 5 of this psalm point back to Adam? How does verse 10 point forward to Christ?

☐ **91:1–16 "In the shadow of the Almighty."**
In what ways is God our "insurance policy"? What is required on our part to be a "policyholder"? (See verse 14.)

☐ **105:1–45 "Remember . . ."**
What things does this psalm exhort Israel to *remember*? How is this psalm a practical teaching as well as an expression of worship?

☐ **120:1–134:3 The Songs of Ascents**
These psalms were sung by Israelites as they traveled to Jerusalem for the annual festivals. Try to imagine yourself walking up toward Jerusalem as you read these fifteen short psalms.

☐ **139:1–24 "Search me, O God, and know my heart."**
What does David realize about God's knowledge of him? Does David feel comfortable in the presence of God's "all-seeing eye"? How sincerely can you echo David's words?

☐ **148:1–150:6 "Praise the Lord!"**
How are these last three psalms a fitting climax to the book of Psalms?

WEEK 5

(Proverbs) Wisdom for Everyday Life

God provided priests to lead his people in worship, and prophets to call them to repentance; he also provided men with godly wisdom to teach them about the practical matters of everyday life.

☐ **Prov. 1:1–33 The key to wisdom.**
For what purposes were these proverbs recorded? What must precede true wisdom (7)?

☐ **4:1–27 The importance of seeking wisdom.**
What should be our attitude toward gaining wisdom? How does the life of the righteous differ from the life of the wicked (18–19)?

☐ **5:1–23; 6:20–7:27 The foolishness of adultery.**
What vivid images describe the folly of adultery? How is 7:27 a fitting summary of this theme?

How can you apply the wisdom of the following passages to your own life:

☐ **11:1–31**

☐ **17:1–28**

☐ **27:1–27**

☐ **31:10–31 The Wife of Noble Character.**
How is the ideal wife described here similar to, or different from, the ideal wife of today? How should a husband treat such a wife (30–31)?

WEEK 6

(Job) The Problem of Human Suffering

If God is good and all-powerful, why is his creation so full of pain and suffering? That is the question Job is faced with when his own life suddenly falls apart. Job's friends are all ready with their answers to that question, but ultimately the only satisfactory answer comes from God himself.

☐ **Job 1:1–2:13 Satan is allowed to test Job.**
What kind of man is Job, according to 1:8? How does God allow Satan to test Job? How does Job respond?

☐ **3:1–26 Job despairs of life.**
Even as Job sinks into despair, does he remain true to his statements in 1:21 and 2:10? Did he ever blame God? (See 1:22.)

☐ **8:1–22 Bildad says Job is suffering because of his sins.**
What way out of suffering does Bildad offer Job? How must Job have felt about Bildad's advice?

☐ **22:1–30 Eliphaz, too, says Job is suffering for his sins.**
Eliphaz gets more specific than Bildad, accusing Job of specific sins which Job later denies (29:11–17). How must Job have felt about Eliphaz's advice in verse 21?

☐ **31:1–40 Job declares his innocence.**
Job examines his life and very specifically defends himself against his friends' accusations. But do the words of 1:22 still hold true of him?

☐ **38:1–41; 40:1–24 God reveals his glory to Job.**
God finally speaks, with questions instead of answers—questions designed to show Job how limited human knowledge is, and how useless it is to question God's ways. Does Job get the message? (See 40:3–5.)

☐ **41:1–42:17 Job acknowledges God's glory.**
In the end, Job's new awareness of God's glory seems to totally eclipse his preoccupation with his suffering. Does this provide a key to dealing with suffering in your own life?

WEEK 7

(Jonah, Hosea, Amos) Israel Called to Repentance

We now go back to Israel's history—specifically the prophets God had sent to warn his people of the final defeats recorded in 2 Kings. Hosea compares Israel's sins against God to the sins of an adulterous wife. Amos speaks out against social injustice. Jonah actually prophesies to Israel's enemies, the Assyrians, calling them to turn to Israel's God.

☐ **Jonah 1:1–2:10 Jonah is a reluctant prophet.**
What is Jonah's initial reaction to God's call to him to prophesy? How does an unusual experience change his mind?

☐ **3:1–4:11 Jonah's success makes him angry.**
Why was Jonah angry when Ninevah repented? How does God teach him the right attitude? How does 4:11 show that God was concerned for all mankind, not just his chosen people?

☐ **Hos. 1:1–3:5 Hosea's adulterous wife.**
How was Hosea's marriage to Gomer to be an example to Israel? How did Hosea show that he loved Gomer in spite of her adultery?

☐ **4:1–19 God's adulterous nation.**
How does Hosea say that Israel has "committed adultery" against God?

☐ **11:1–14:9 God wants his people to repent.**
What do we learn here about God's love for his people? About his high expectations of them? About his willingness to forgive?

☐ **Amos 5:1–6:14 Israel fails to pursue justice.**
What specific examples does Amos give of Israel's failure to pursue social justice? How does this make God feel about their religious observances (21–24)?

☐ **9:1–15 Israel will be destroyed, and restored.**
What is the "bad news" and "good news" of this chapter?

WEEK 8

(Isaiah) Salvation for All Mankind

Isaiah's long ministry ended during the time of Judah's righteous king Hezekiah (2 Kings 18–19). Isaiah sees what has happened to the northern kingdom, and predicts that Judah will suffer the same fate, but will eventually be restored to its land. Looking even farther, he sees that God will one day bring salvation to all mankind.

☐ **Isa. 6:1–7:17; 9:1–7 Isaiah's call and early prophecies.**
What is Isaiah's attitude when God calls him? What two mentions of the coming Messiah do we find in these passages?

☐ **36:1–37:38 The historical context of Isaiah.**
Notice that the events and prophecies of these chapters duplicate 2 Kings 18 and 19. This should help you place Isaiah in his historical context.

☐ **40:1–31 "Comfort my people."**
Chapters 40 through 66 are, for the most part, words of comfort and hope. How does the picture of mankind in 6–8 contrast with that of 30–31? What makes the difference?

☐ **51:1–23 Israel will return from exile.**
What picture of Israel's captured land is presented in 1–3? What will happen to the people in exile? What will happen to their captors?

☐ **52:1–53:12 The Suffering Servant.**
How does 52:1–12 prepare us for the wonderful prophecy to follow? What will the Messiah be like? How did Christ fulfill these prophecies?

☐ **55:1–56:8 God's invitation to all mankind.**
What does this passage invite us to do? What verses indicate that this invitation is for all mankind, not just for Israel?

☐ **65:17–25 New heavens and a new earth.**
What symbols does Isaiah use to express what eternal life will be like? How does his description compare to Rev. 21–22?

WEEK 9

(Jeremiah) Warnings of Judah's Destruction

Jeremiah's ministry follows that of Isaiah; in fact, he warns of Judah's fate right up to when it finally falls and goes into exile. When Jeremiah isn't "doing time" in prison because of his prophecies, he is actively involved in the reform movements that precede Judah's fall.

☐ **Jer. 1:1–19 Jeremiah is called to prophesy.**
How is Jeremiah's response to his call similar to that of Moses and Gideon? What does this passage suggest about Jeremiah's age at that time?

☐ **7:1–29 Judah's religious hypocrisy.**
What kind of picture does Jeremiah paint of the nation's spiritual health? What especially upsets him (9–11)?

☐ **18:1–19:15 The potter and the clay.**
What powerful object lesson does Jeremiah teach using clay? How is God like the potter? How is Israel like the clay?

☐ **26:1–24 Jeremiah is threatened with death.**
Why did the people want to kill Jeremiah? How did he "get off the hook" this time?

☐ **30:1–24 Israel will be restored!**
How bad is Israel's spiritual sickness (12)? What is the only possible cure? (See 30:18.)

☐ **37:1–38:28 Jeremiah is imprisoned, and thrown into a cistern.**
In light of what happens to Jeremiah in these two chapters, what is ironic about the request in 37:3? What did Jeremiah urge the people to do, right up to the very end (20)?

☐ **39:1–40:6 The fall of Jerusalem.**
As Jerusalem was being led captive, what was Jeremiah's fate? What must his former tormentors have thought of him now?

144

WEEK 10

(Daniel) A Prophet in Exile

Daniel was among those taken captive to Babylon in 605 B.C., nineteen years before the final fall of Jerusalem. In Babylon he takes a stand for God's laws amid an alien culture. God grants Daniel many visions about future events, showing him again and again that God is ultimately in control of human history.

☐ **Dan. 1:1–21 Daniel is faithful to his God.**
How did Daniel honor God amid this alien culture? How did God in turn honor him? What was his reputation among his captors?

☐ **2:1–49 Daniel interprets the king's dream.**
How is Daniel's faith shown as he faces this challenge? Why are Daniel's actions in 27–28 so courageous and admirable?

☐ **3:1–30 The fiery furnace**
How challenging was it to live as a believer in God while in Babylon? What "images of gold" are Christians today pressured to worship?

☐ **4:1–37 God rules over the kingdoms of man.**
God actually uses King Nebuchadnezzar to state the theme of this book. What is it (17)? How does he learn that truth in an unforgettable way?

☐ **6:1–28 Daniel is thrown into a den of lions.**
What actions lead to Daniel's being thrown into the lions' den? How might we face a similar challenge today? What might be the result of our taking a stand for God as Daniel did?

☐ **7:1–28 Daniel's vision of the four beasts.**
What is the ultimate fate of the four empires Daniel dreams about? How does this prove the truth of what Nebuchadnezzar realized in chapter 4?

☐ **9:1–19 Daniel prays for his people.**
What is Daniel's great desire for his people Israel? On what historic event does he base his hope? How does the angel Gabriel respond to Daniel's pleas (21–27)?

WEEK 11

(Esther) A Woman's Courage Saves the Nation

Esther is a Jewish exile in Persia, which had conquered Babylon. Her story begins about fifty years after the close of Daniel's record, which is also about fifty years after the first group of exiles returned to Jerusalem. Her courageous actions save the Jews remaining in Persia from extermination, making possible the second return reported by Ezra and Nehemiah.

☐ **Est. 1:1–2:23 Esther becomes queen.**
Describe the strange course of events that allows Esther, a Jew, to providentially become queen of Persia.

☐ **3:1–15 Haman plots genocide.**
What insult provokes Haman to plan the extermination of all the Jews in Persia? How does he persuade the king to go along with him? What edict is issued (3:13)?

☐ **4:1–17 Esther is asked to intervene.**
If all the Jews *had* been exterminated, would Queen Esther have died along with them? (See 2:20.) Describe her courage, her sense of destiny and duty as she decides to approach the king.

☐ **5:1–14 Esther's first request to the king.**
Why do you suppose Esther delays in requesting that her people be spared? (We'll see shortly how providential the delay was.) What does Haman do that he'll soon regret?

☐ **6:1–7:10 A providential turn of events!**
Did a simple case of insomnia play a decisive role in the fate of the Jews? How does Haman get his "just deserts" for his hatred and pride?

☐ **8:1–17 The Jews are granted the right to defend themselves.**
By Persian custom, the edict of 3:13 couldn't be canceled; but in answer to Esther's request a second edict was issued allowing the Jews to arm themselves against those who would try to carry out the first edict.

☐ **9:1–10:3 The Jews are triumphant.**
How did Mordecai's influence help the Jews win the battles of chapter 9? To what is Mordecai's greatness attributed (10:3)?

WEEK 12

(Ezra, Nehemiah) The Exiles Return

It has been twenty-five years since Esther saved the Jews in exile, and seventy-five years since the first exiles had returned to Jerusalem. Ezra now leads a second group of returnees, and brings a much-needed spiritual revival to the wayward veterans of the earlier return. Nehemiah continues the revival as he spearheads the rebuilding of Jerusalem's walls.

☐ **Ezra 1:1–11; 2:68–3:13 The first group of exiles return.**
What various emotions do these returning exiles feel as reconstruction begins on the temple?

☐ **4:1–6:22 Opposition to rebuilding the temple.**
How does 4:4–5 reveal the hypocrisy of what the enemies of Judah had claimed in 4:2? How do the Jews initially react to the opposition (4:24)? How do they finally finish the task?

☐ **7:1–28; 8:15–36 Ezra leads the second group of returnees.**
What kind of person is Ezra? How does his good reputation in Persia enable him to lead the returning exiles? How does he provide spiritual leadership on the journey to Jerusalem?

☐ **Neh. 1:1–2:20 Nehemiah wants to rebuild Jerusalem's walls.**
What distressing news does Nehemiah hear about Jerusalem? What specific need does he take on as his special project?

☐ **4:1–23 The walls are rebuilt, despite opposition.**
Describe the "working conditions" as Jerusalem's walls are rebuilt.

☐ **8:1–9:38 Ezra reads the law; the people repent.**
How do the people respond when the Law is read to them? How do they express this by their actions? How does 9:33 summarize the Levites' prayer of repentance?

☐ **13:1–31 Nehemiah's final reforms.**
What specific sins had become widespread among these returned exiles? What does this suggest they had learned from the judgment and exile God had brought upon their nation?

WEEK 13

(Haggai, Zechariah, Malachi) Keep the Faith!

Haggai and Zechariah were among the first group of returning exiles. They spoke words of encouragement as the people rebuilt the city. Zechariah often looked farther into the future, to the time when the Messiah would come. Malachi, writing nearly a hundred years later, closes the Old Testament with one last call to repentance.

☐ Hag. 1:1–2:23 Finish rebuilding the temple!
How does Haggai's rebuke (1:1–11) "hit close to home"? How does he encourage the "older" people we read about in Ezra 3:12?

☐ Zech. 1:1–17 "My house will be rebuilt!"
How do the people respond to Zechariah's first message? What does God promise about the work of reconstruction they have begun?

☐ 7:1–13 A call for justice.
What does Zechariah say about the connection between worshiping God and promoting social justice? Compare this passage to Amos 5:1–6:14 and Jer. 7:9–11.

☐ 8:1–23 Jerusalem's future greatness.
How does God feel about Jerusalem? What do his future plans for Jerusalem include?

☐ 9:1–17 The king is coming!
Looking further into Israel's future, what does Zechariah see?

☐ Mal. 1:1–2:16 One last call to repentance.
What are some of the sins still plaguing Israel, some hundred years after they returned from exile? What is one result of their sin (2:9)?

☐ 2:17–4:6 The day of the Lord.
What references to Christ do we find in these final words of the Old Testament? Is the very last word of the Old Testament a good summary of its content? How does that word point forward to the New Testament?

3rd Quarter:
Matthew–Acts

WEEK 1

(Gospels) The Birth of Jesus the Messiah

It has been four hundred years since Malachi's last call to repentance. The nation has sinned again and is now ruled by Rome; they are awaiting a leader who will deliver them from this foreign domination. But Jesus Christ will offer them liberation of a different kind. (Our survey of the Gospels will draw from Matthew, Luke, and John.)

☐ **Luke 1:1–38 Angels appear to Zechariah and Mary.**
What similarity is there in the way that Zechariah and Mary respond to the angels' messages? After her initial surprise, what is Mary's attitude?

☐ **1:39–56 Mary visits Elizabeth.**
How would you describe Mary's attitude in this passage? For what does she express thanks in her song? How does Jesus fulfill her words?

☐ **1:57–80 The birth of John the Baptist.**
Do the people of John's town realize there is something special about him? How well does Zechariah understand what Jesus will do?

☐ **2:1–20 The birth of Jesus.**
What details of this story assure us that it is not just a myth? How would you describe the surroundings in which Jesus is born?

☐ **2:21–40 Jesus is presented at the temple.**
What feelings do Simeon and Anna experience upon seeing the baby Jesus?

☐ **Matt. 2:1–12 The visit of the Magi.**
By what two means are the Magi from the east made aware of the importance of Christ's birth? How does God protect Jesus from Herod?

☐ **2:13–23 The escape to Egypt.**
How is God's protection continued in these verses? What three prophecies are fulfilled here?

WEEK 2

(Gospels) John's Report of Jesus' Early Ministry

While the three other Gospel accounts cover many events in Jesus' life, John, writing years later, focuses on just a few events and thoroughly explores the significance of each. John begins his Gospel by firmly establishing the fact that Jesus is more than just a remarkable human being.

☐ **John 1:1–18 Jesus was there before the beginning.**
What is Jesus' relationship to God? What was his role in creation? How does Israel respond to their Messiah? How does Jesus bridge the gap between God and mankind?

☐ **1:19–36 The testimony of John the Baptist.**
How does John compare his own ministry to that of Jesus? How does God assure John of Jesus' divine nature? How does John in turn testify to Jesus' divine nature?

☐ **1:37–51 Disciples begin to follow Jesus.**
How do John's disciples react to his statement in verse 36? How is Jesus' divine nature revealed in his encounter with Nathanael?

☐ **2:1–12 Jesus turns water into wine.**
What does this miracle show about Jesus' concern for the ordinary needs of people? How does the miracle affect Jesus' disciples?

☐ **2:13–25 Jesus clears the temple of moneychangers.**
How do Jesus' disciples respond to his clearing the temple? When did the miracle Jesus promised in verse 19 take place? What effect did it have then?

☐ **3:1–21 The new birth.**
What draws Nicodemus to Jesus? What does Jesus say is necessary for eternal life (3)? How does Jesus say this new birth can occur (16)?

☐ **3:22–36 John the Baptist's further testimony about Jesus.**
What was John's view of his own ministry, now that Jesus' ministry had begun? How does John's statement in verse 36 echo the words of Jesus?

WEEK 3

(Gospels) What Jesus Said About Himself

Jesus of Nazareth went about the business of everyday life much like the other people of his day. But he claimed to be much more than a mere human. And he backed up his supernatural claims with supernatural actions. Let's look at some of the "I am's" of John's Gospel.

☐ **John 4:4–42 "I who speak to you am he."**
What originally impressed the Samaritan woman about Jesus? What supernatural "sign" did Jesus perform to back up his claim in verse 26? How did the woman respond?

☐ **6:1–60 "I am the bread of life."**
How does Jesus use a miracle to teach his followers about himself? Do his disciples and other listeners understand what he is saying?

☐ **8:12–41 "I am the light of the world."**
Who does Jesus "call as a witness" in his behalf (18)? What does Jesus warn will be the consequence of not believing in him?

☐ **8:48–59 "Before Abraham was born, I am."**
What is the opinion of many who do not believe in Jesus? What quality does Jesus claim to possess in verse 58?

☐ **9:1–41 "I am the light of the world."**
What spiritual effect does this miracle have on the blind man? On the Pharisees? What does Jesus say about the Pharisees in verse 41?

☐ **10:1–21 "I am the good shepherd."**
With what two "I am" statements does Jesus illustrate his loving concern for his followers? How do you explain the sharp division of opinion about Jesus (19–21)?

☐ **11:1–44 "I am the resurrection and the life."**
What in this story shows that Jesus is fully human? What shows that he is fully God?

WEEK 4

(Gospels) The Sermon on the Mount

Jesus now talks with his followers about the moral principles that should guide their everyday living. He makes it clear that he is not setting aside the teachings of Moses, but rather is clarifying the heart attitudes that should undergird obedience to the Law.

☐ **Matt. 5:1–12 The Beatitudes.**
What sorts of things should make a disciple of Jesus "blessed," or happy? How well will such a person fit in with the unbelieving world?

☐ **5:13–26 Salt and light.**
In what practical ways can we apply the teaching of 13–14? How can our righteousness surpass that of the Pharisees (20)? How do 21–48 help answer that question?

☐ **5:27–48 Attitudes of the heart.**
In what ways does Jesus show that attitudes are more important, and harder to control, than actions?

☐ **6:1–18 Doing good anonymously.**
Why does Jesus want us to be so secretive about things like fasting, prayer, and giving to the needy? In all three cases, what recognition will we receive?

☐ **6:19–34 Treasures in heaven.**
What happens when we try to "serve two masters" (24)? What are the two masters we would likely try to serve? How does Jesus' way of handling wealth reduce worry?

☐ **7:1–14 "Judge not."**
Why is it so inappropriate for us to be judging other people? How does Jesus reassure us that God will answer our prayers?

☐ **7:15–29 The house built on the rock.**
Will the heart attitudes Jesus has talked about result in righteous actions (17)? What danger faces those who agree with Jesus' teachings, but don't let it affect their lives?

WEEK 5

(Gospels) Encounters With Jesus

A great teacher can be impressive delivering an oration in front of a crowd, and yet be a failure in everyday relationships. How does Jesus appear to those who chance to encounter him on the streets and in the marketplaces of ancient Palestine? How does he come across in "life's unguarded moments"?

☐ **Matt. 9:9–17 Associating with sinners.**
What do the righteous people of Jesus' day think of his choice of friends?

☐ **12:1–14 Lord of the Sabbath.**
What does this incident show about Christ's compassion for human need?

☐ **18:1–10; 19:13–15; 21:15–16 Jesus and the little children.**
Why did Jesus have such a special concern for children? How do you suppose they responded to him?

☐ **Luke 9:10–17 Jesus welcomes an interruption.**
How does Jesus respond to the unplanned event of verse 11? How does he then "go the second mile"?

☐ **John 8:1–11 Jesus and the adulterous woman.**
How do the Pharisees *expect* Jesus to respond to the woman taken in adultery? How does he use the situation to teach them a lesson?

☐ **13:1–17 Jesus washes his disciples' feet.**
Why, according to verse 1, does Jesus wash the disciples' feet at this time? What are some ways we can follow his example (15) today?

☐ **19:16–27 Jesus' concern for his mother.**
Why is Jesus' action in 26–27 so remarkable in light of when it occurred?

WEEK 6

(Gospels) The Miracles of Jesus

Jesus performs miracles both to *show* who he is, and *because of* who he is. We saw in John's Gospel how his miracles become occasions for validating his ministry. But his miracles also grow out of compassion for helpless mankind (Matt. 14:14). Even after boldly declaring "I am the resurrection," he turns aside and weeps before raising Lazarus.

☐ **Matt. 14:13–33 Feeding five thousand; walking on water.**
Should Peter have been afraid (28–31) in light of what he had witnessed earlier that day (13–21)? Would you have been afraid?

☐ **Luke 5:1–11 Catching fish, and disciples.**
What makes Peter, James, and John so ready to make a "mid-life career change?"

☐ **5:17–26 Bold faith leads to a healing.**
What impresses Jesus about the paralytic and his friends? How do the Pharisees provide Jesus an opportunity to prove his deity?

☐ **7:1–23 A Roman centurion's request.**
How is the centurion's faith greater than that of most people Jesus encountered (9)? Note, in verse 16, that Jesus doesn't have to say anything about his deity—the people say it for him!

☐ **17:11–19 The ten lepers.**
What does Jesus note about the one grateful leper? Why must this have disappointed him? What does the nine-to-one ratio suggest about human nature?

☐ **John 4:46–54 The miracle was right on time!**
What especially impresses the royal official about this miracle? What is his response?

☐ **5:1–47 Miracles and other proofs of Jesus' deity.**
How is Jesus' offer of eternal life (24) validated by what he has just done? What three other things, besides his miracles, does Jesus say prove who he is (31–40)?

WEEK 7

(Gospels) The Parables of Jesus

When a teacher wants to convey important information, it is customary to organize that information in outline form and deliver it as a lecture. But a large part of Jesus' public teaching is in the form of parables, simple stories of everyday life that revealed deep spiritual truth to those ready to receive it (see Matt. 13:10–17).

☐ **Matt. 13:1–52 Parables of the kingdom.**
How does each of these parables show the importance of our individual response to the gospel?

☐ **20:1–16 Workers in the vineyard.**
What does the equal pay these men receive represent? How does verse 16 compare to the world's way of doing things?

☐ **25:1–46 Be ready!**
How does each of these three parables stress the importance of living in such a way that we are ready for Christ's return?

☐ **Luke 11:1–13 Prayer: an example and a parable.**
What important truth about prayer is Jesus able to make in this parable that he couldn't have made just by the example he gives?

☐ **12:13–21 The rich fool.**
How does this parable illustrate the theme stated in verse 15? How can we be "rich toward God"?

☐ **14:1–24 The great banquet.**
What prompts Jesus to tell this parable? How are the banquet's "no-shows" typical of those who reject the gospel? How are the "crippled, blind, and lame" typical of those who accept the gospel?

☐ **15:1–32 Three lost things.**
What prompts Jesus to tell these parables? Who do you suppose is his "target audience"?

WEEK 8

(Gospels) Final Teachings and Prayers of Jesus

As Jesus faces the final hours of his earthly life, he focuses his attention on those who have been his closest followers. He assures them that his impending death will not be the end, and that the ministry for which they have sacrificed everything will continue under the guidance of the Holy Spirit.

☐ **John 14:1–31 Words of comfort and hope.**
What does Jesus say he'll be doing for his disciples after he leaves them? What will the Holy Spirit do for the disciples?

☐ **15:1–17 The vine and the branches.**
Explain in your own words how Christ is like a vine and we are like branches on that vine.

☐ **15:18–27 "If the world hates you . . ."**
Why does the world hate true followers of Jesus?

☐ **16:1–15 The ministry of the Holy Spirit.**
How will the Holy Spirit "minister" to non-Christians? To Christians?

☐ **16:16–33 "I will see you again."**
What common human experience does Jesus use to explain the great sorrow, followed by great joy, of his death and resurrection? How does this passage end on a "down note" (31)?

☐ **17:1–26 Final prayers.**
Match these three prayer requests: a) unity; b) protection; c) glorification; with these three groups Jesus prayed for: a) himself; b) his disciples; c) future believers.

☐ **Luke 22:39–46 The prayer in Gethsemane.**
John 18:1 reports that Jesus then went to Gethsemane; Luke tells the story from there. What does this passage say about Christ's being fully human as well as fully divine? (See Heb. 4:15.)

WEEK 9

(Gospels)   The Betrayal and Trial of Jesus

Jesus' final days involve many betrayals: the actual conspiracy between Judas and the Jewish leaders; the fickleness of the crowds shouting "Hosanna" and then just hours later calling for his crucifixion; the sudden desertion of all his closest friends. But through it all, Jesus is faithful in preparing to face the painful and lonely death for which he was born.

☐ **John 11:45–57 The religious leaders plot to kill Jesus.**
What wonderful event is the immediate provocation for the plot to kill Jesus? What do you suppose motivates Jesus to withdraw from public ministry at this time (54)?

☐ **12:1–36 The triumphal entry.**
How well do you think the crowds in 12–13 understand the mission of Jesus? What warning does Jesus give the crowds in 34–36?

☐ **Luke 21:5–38 Jesus talks about the end times.**
What does Jesus warn the future holds for his followers? What is to be their attitude amid all that will happen (36)? What will be the final outcome (31)?

☐ **22:7–38 The Last Supper.**
Besides being the "Last Supper" Jesus shares with his disciples, why is it also the last time they will need to celebrate the Passover (see 16)?

☐ **John 13:12–38 Jesus predicts his betrayal.**
What does verse 21 suggest about Jesus' *feelings* as he predicts his betrayal? Describe how Peter might have been feeling in 36–38.

☐ **18:1–27 Jesus is arrested.**
What do Jesus' statements in verses 8 and 11 say about his character? What does the contrast in Peter's action in verse 10 and his later denial say about *his* character?

☐ **18:28–40 He stands trial before Pilate.**
What is the irony of the Jews' actions in verse 28? Does Pilate understand why Jesus has been arrested? What might Pilate have meant by his question in verse 38?

WEEK 10

(Gospels) The Death and Resurrection of Jesus

Pilate hands Jesus back over to the Jews; again they demand crucifixion and the Roman authorities carry out that sentence. Jesus dies on the cross and is buried. His enemies breathe a sigh of relief. But then things start to happen; we'll need the help of three eyewitnesses, Matthew, Luke, and John, to piece together the exciting events of the next few days.

☐ **John 19:1–16 Jesus receives the death sentence.**
What is the charge against Jesus (7)? Besides Jesus' mere words, why do the Jewish leaders want to get rid of him (see 11:45–48)? Who actually condemns Jesus to die—Pilate or the Jews?

☐ **19:17–42 The crucifixion and burial.**
How does God use Pilate to proclaim the truth about Jesus (19–22)? How does the crucifixion validate Pilate's proclamation? (See 2 Sam. 7:12–16).

☐ **Matt. 28:1–15 Resurrection!**
Where is Jesus when the angel rolls back the stone? How is the angels' report verified? What does it take to deny the fact of the Resurrection?

☐ **Luke 24:13–35 On the road to Emmaus.**
Are the rumors of Jesus' resurrection (22–24) enough to rekindle the faith of the disciples? How do they finally realize that Jesus has risen?

☐ **John 20:19-21:14 Further appearances of the risen Christ.**
What do the events of 20:19–29 tell us about Christ's resurrected body? How does Jesus show his love for his disciples in 21:1–14?

☐ **21:15–25 Peter is reinstated.**
Why do you suppose Jesus singles Peter out for special attention?

☐ **Luke 24:36–53 The Ascension.**
Again we have some hints as to the nature of Christ's resurrected body (36–39). Try to imagine how he "was taken up into heaven" (51).

WEEK 11

(Acts) The Church Is Born

Luke adds to his account of Jesus' life an account of the church he established (see Matt. 16:18) to proclaim salvation to all mankind (Acts 1:8). In Acts we'll see clear testimony that Christ did, in truth, rise from the dead. For the band of fearful disciples who had deserted him, and concluded that his death was the end, are now ready to turn the world upside down.

☐ **Acts 1:1–26 Jesus commissions his disciples.**
What does Jesus say will shortly happen (8)? What will this enable his disciples to do (8)? Does this fuller description of the Ascension (9–10) match how you imagined it?

☐ **2:1–47 The baptism of the Holy Spirit.**
What miracle validated the new role of the Holy Spirit? To whom does Peter shift the main focus (22–36)? How do the people respond? How does their response take on a permanent form?

☐ **3:1–26 The ministry of Peter.**
What does Peter do as soon as the miracle gets the people's attention?

☐ **4:1–37 Miracles + preaching = church growth.**
How do the Jewish leaders react to the message and miracle of Peter and John? How do the people respond? How do verses 32–36 show the sincerity of the people's faith?

☐ **6:8–8:3 The testimony and death of Stephen.**
What about Stephen's speech would have made his Jewish audience so angry? Do you suppose Saul's actions in 8:3 are in response to Stephen's remarks?

☐ **9:1–31 The conversion of Saul.**
Why does it take supernatural intervention to bring Saul to faith? How does Saul demonstrate the genuineness of his conversion? What does God say will be his special mission (9:15)?

☐ **10:1–48 The conversion of Cornelius.**
What does it take to convince these Jewish believers in Christ that the gospel is for Gentiles as well?

WEEK 12

(Acts) Paul's Missionary Journeys

Having spent several years in quiet preparation, Saul (now known as Paul) begins in earnest his special assignment of proclaiming to the Gentile world the gospel he once so bitterly opposed. That he is truly God's "chosen instrument" (9:15) for this task will become abundantly clear as we follow him throughout the Roman empire.

☐ **Acts 13:1–52 Paul's first missionary journey.**
How is Paul's sermon to the Jews (14-41) similar to Stephen's (chapter 7)? How is the response similar? What does Paul then announce (46–52)?

☐ **14:1–28 Ministry in Asia Minor.**
How do the people of Lystra respond to the miracle Paul performs? What is Paul's response? Why do Paul and Barnabas retrace their steps (21–28)?

☐ **15:36–16:40 The second journey.**
How do Paul and Silas end up in jail? What is the eventual outcome of their imprisonment?

☐ **17:1–34 Ministry in Greece.**
What kind of audience does Paul find at Berea? How does Paul explain the "Unknown God" to the people of Athens?

☐ **18:1–22 Trouble in Corinth.**
How do the Jews in Corinth respond to Paul? How do they interfere with Paul's ministry to the Gentiles there?

☐ **18:23–19:41 The third journey.**
What key role is played by Priscilla and Aquila? What goes into the bonfire in 19:18–20? Who is upset about it (23–28)? How is this similar to what happened at Philippi (16:16–24)?

☐ **20:1–38 Farewell to Ephesus.**
Why is Paul not afraid to go to Jerusalem (22–24)? What does the emotional scene in 36–38 say about his ministry?

WEEK 13

(Acts) Paul's Ministry in Jerusalem and Rome

God had said that Paul would "carry my name before the Gentiles and their kings" (9:15). We have seen Paul's ministry to the Gentiles throughout the Roman empire; we will now see him providentially finding opportunities to bear witness to Christ before its rulers.

☐ **Acts 21:1–36 Paul arrested in Jerusalem.**
What further warning does Paul have about impending trouble in Jerusalem? Who instigates Paul's arrest? Why?

☐ **21:37–22:29 Paul tells of his conversion.**
At what point in Paul's speech does his Jewish audience turn against him? What saves Paul from being beaten?

☐ **22:30–23:35 Paul before the Sanhedrin.**
How do events lead to Paul's being able to appear before Roman leaders?

☐ **24:1–25:22 Paul stands trial twice; appeals to Caesar.**
How does Paul use his appearances before Felix? Why does Paul appeal his case to Caesar (25:10–11)? (See Rom. 1:10.)

☐ **25:23–26:32 Paul before Agrippa.**
Do you think Agrippa and the others who heard Paul knew the facts of Jesus' ministry and resurrection? (See 26:26.)

☐ **27:1–28:15 Paul is taken to Rome.**
How is Paul able to share the gospel with people he is with on the way to Rome?

☐ **28:16–31 Paul's ministry in Rome.**
How does Paul use his time in Rome? Do you think Paul was ever able to witness directly to Caesar? (See Phil. 1:13 and 4:22.)

4th Quarter:
Romans–Revelation

WEEK 1

(Romans) The Good News of God's Grace in Christ

Paul's letter to Rome has been called "the Gospel according to Paul." It is the Bible's most thorough and systematic presentation of the plan of salvation. In the first seven chapters Paul shows that sin is a universal problem—a problem without solution except for the solution God has provided in Jesus Christ.

☐ **Rom. 1:1–32 Mankind stands guilty before God.**
What does Paul say is obvious to all people (18–32)? Why do we deny what is obvious? What is the result of our denial?

☐ **2:1–3:8 Even "good" people are guilty.**
What does Paul say about people who seem to be morally good?

☐ **3:9–31 The good news of God's grace.**
What is the "bad news" and "good news" in this passage? Could verses 23–24 be considered a summary of the entire Bible?

☐ **4:1–25 Even Abraham was saved by grace.**
How did Abraham, and David, experience God's grace in their lives?

☐ **5:1–21 The blessings of grace.**
What characteristics does God's grace produce in our lives? What contrasts does Paul make between Christ and Adam?

☐ **6:1–7:6 We are dead to sin, alive in Christ.**
Why is it so inappropriate for a Christian to go on living the way he or she did before being saved?

☐ **7:7–25 But we still sometimes struggle with sin.**
Do you have the same struggle with sin that Paul had? Paul briefly states the solution to this struggle in 24–25, then more fully in chapter 8.

WEEK 2

(Romans) Grace at Work

Having described the agony of the soul weighed down by sin, Paul now describes in chapter 8 the joy of the soul fully aware of salvation in Christ. In chapters 9–11 he explains how God's grace is at work in Israel and the rest of the human race. Then in the remaining chapters he shows some of the practical ways grace should be expressed in each of our lives.

☐ **Rom. 8:1–17 Life through the Holy Spirit.**
How does Paul say we, as Christians, can experience victory in our battle with our sinful nature?

☐ **8:18–39 More than conquerors.**
How does the future we as Christians can look forward to compare with what we may have to endure in the present? How secure should God's love make us feel (31–39)?

☐ **9:1–29 Why did Israel reject the gospel?**
If God chose the Jews to bring Christ to the world, why did most of them reject him? Paul begins to answer that question by declaring that God is right even when his plans don't make sense to us.

☐ **9:30–10:21 Israel is responsible for its actions.**
Even though God may have known that Israel would reject Christ, says Paul, Israel must still bear responsibility for that rejection. They cannot blame their sin on God.

☐ **11:1–36 *Some* Jews, and *some* Gentiles, will be saved.**
Paul then shows that both Jews and Gentiles who believe in Christ will be saved, and that each has a unique part in God's plan. How does his "olive tree" illustration (17–21) show this?

☐ **12:1–15:13 Grace at work in our lives.**
How should the great truths Paul has explained in Romans help to "renew" our minds and "transform" our lives (12:2)? How should grace affect the various relationships Paul talks about.

☐ **15:14–16:27 Final exhortations and greetings.**
How would God's unusual answer to the Roman Christians' prayer in 15:31 lead to an answer to Paul's longing in 15:23–24? (See Acts 25–27.)

WEEK 3

(1 Corinthians) A Young Church With Problems

Paul had established a church in Corinth (Acts 18:1–18). But very soon there were serious problems among these new believers. Paul writes this letter to address these problems, and to better establish the Corinthians in their faith.

☐ **1 Cor. 1:1–2:16 Worldly wisdom vs. godly wisdom.**
What is the problem addressed in 1:1–17? What answer does Paul present in 1:18–2:16? What are some differences between worldly wisdom and the wisdom God gives?

☐ **5:1–6:19 Our faith should affect the way we live.**
How would you describe the Corinthians' level of spiritual maturity? How does Paul say the Christian lifestyle should differ from that of the world?

☐ **7:1–40 Our faith should affect our view of marriage.**
How does the phrase "the time is short" (29) provide a theme for what Paul says about marriage among Christians?

☐ **9:1–27 What motivates Paul to preach.**
What "compels" Paul (16) to preach the gospel and give up so many of life's comforts? (See 2 Cor. 5:14.) How does Paul urge the Corinthians to follow his example?

☐ **12:1–31 Christians should all work together.**
How is the church like a human body? What is the common goal of each part of the body or church?

☐ **13:1–13 Love is the greatest!**
Why is love greater than any "gift" a Christian might possess? How have you seen the characteristics of love (4–7) demonstrated in people's lives?

☐ **15:1–58 Christ has risen, and so will we!**
Why is belief in Christ's resurrection absolutely essential to Christian faith? What does Christ's resurrection say about our own future as Christians?

WEEK 4

(2 Corinthians) Paul Defends His Ministry

Paul's ministry in Corinth had been so difficult that Christ appeared to him in a dream to encourage him (Acts 18:9). And in 1 Corinthians we saw a church riddled with problems. Now in this second letter Paul must defend his very right to be an apostle. Still, his letter is filled with words of encouragement and inspiration for this struggling church.

☐ **2 Cor. 1:1–3:18 Words of encouragement.**
What is Paul's attitude toward suffering (1:3–11)? How does he compare the gospel to the Law of Moses (3:7–18)?

☐ **4:1–18 Treasures in jars of clay.**
How are we like jars of clay? As such, what is our source of hope?

☐ **5:1–6:2 The ministry of reconciliation.**
What should be the primary life-goal of a Christian (1–10)? In light of this, how should we relate to non-Christians (11–21)?

☐ **6:3–7:16 Paul's hardships, and joy.**
What kinds of things did Paul endure for the Corinthians? How were they a source of joy to him in spite of all the troubles?

☐ **8:1–9:15 Our giving, God's giving.**
How does Paul speak of our giving to God (8:1–15; 9:1–5) in comparison to God's giving to us (9:6–15)?

☐ **10:1–12:10 Paul defends his ministry.**
How does Paul compare his ministry to that of the "super apostles" (11:5)? According to 11:6, what may have been one way they were considered superior to Paul? (See also 1 Cor. 1:17; 2:1–3.)

☐ **12:10–13:14 Weakness and true strength.**
Where does Paul find his true source of strength?

WEEK 5

(Ephesians) God's Eternal Plan for Us

From his imprisonment in Rome, Paul wrote this letter of comfort and encouragement to the believers in Ephesus. He shows how God's plan of salvation was in place from all eternity past, was fulfilled in Christ, and should now be transforming us into "children of light" amid the darkness of a sinful world.

☐ **Eph. 1:1–23 Predestined for salvation!**
For how long has our salvation as Christians been assured? What is the Holy Spirit's role in this assurance? What do *we* need to do to have this assurance (17–18)?

☐ **2:1–22 Alive in Christ.**
According to verse 8, what is God's role in salvation? What is our role? How should salvation affect social and racial barriers (11–22)?

☐ **3:1–21 Our strength in Christ.**
What should our salvation give us in the midst of suffering (12–13)? What is our source of strength (14–19)?

☐ **4:1–32 Our unity in Christ.**
What should be the characteristics of a life "worthy of the calling" we have as Christians?

☐ **4:17–5:21 Children of Light.**
What kinds of "darkness" are described here? What is the "fruit" of living in the light of Christ?

☐ **5:22–6:9 Christ's light in relationships.**
How does Christian faith affect the marriage relationship? What other relationships should be changed by the gospel?

☐ **6:10–18 "The full armor of God."**
How does each piece of armor Paul describes help us to "stand against the devil's schemes?"

WEEK 6

(Philippians) "Rejoice in the Lord!"

As Paul writes this letter, he is in prison and is facing the real possibility of death, yet throughout the letter he speaks of joy—a joy that can be ours as Christians whether we live or die, and whether our life is one of ease or suffering.

☐ **Phil. 1:1–11 Thankfulness and concern.**
Why is Paul thankful for the Christians in Philippi? What are his concerns for them?

☐ **1:12–30 "Stand firm!"**
How could verse 21 be a "theme verse" for Paul's life? What experience do he and the Philippian Christians have in common (27–30)?

☐ **2:1–11 Imitate Christ's humility.**
How is Christ the supreme example of humility? What did his humility ultimately lead to?

☐ **2:12–30 Shining like stars.**
How could Paul's poetic words in verse 15 be an encouragement to the Philippians?

☐ **3:1–11 "I want to know Christ."**
What things are on the "profit" side of Paul's ledger? On the "loss" side? What is his one goal in life?

☐ **3:12–21 Pressing on toward the goal.**
How does "forgetting what is behind" help us to pursue our goal as Christians? Should we look to anyone besides Christ as an example? (See verse 17.)

☐ **4:1–23 Final words of encouragement.**
What qualities of character does Paul encourage them to pursue? Why does Paul feel especially close to the Philippians?

WEEK 7

(1, 2 Thessalonians) Commendation and Exhortation

Paul was forced to flee Thessalonica due to persecution (Acts 17:1–9). When he later heard that the Christians there were holding up well amid continuing trouble, he wrote his first letter to encourage them and build them up in their faith. He wrote a second letter to further encourage them and clear up some questions about Christ's second coming.

☐ **1 Thess. 1:1–10 "We thank God always for you."**
Why is Paul thankful for the Thessalonians? How have they been an inspiration to other Christians?

☐ **2:1–3:13 Paul's ministry to the Thessalonians.**
What fond memory does Paul have of the Thessalonians' response to his ministry? How does Timothy's report encourage him?

☐ **4:1–12 Lives that are pleasing to God.**
Why would Paul's admonition in 3–8 be so crucial in a pagan society? What kind of "ambitions" should characterize a Christian (11)?

☐ **4:13–5:28 The Second Coming.**
How should Christian funerals be distinctively different from pagan funerals? What should be our attitude as we await Christ's return?

☐ **2 Thess. 1:1–12 Eternal blessings vs. punishment.**
When does Paul say justice will finally prevail? What sharp contrast does he draw in 7–9?

☐ **2:1–17 About the Second Coming.**
What wrong information had upset the Thessalonians? What are they instructed to do until the Lord returns?

☐ **3:1–18 Concluding remarks.**
What is Paul's overall feeling about the Thessalonians? What is his attitude toward the lazy people among them?

WEEK 8

(1, 2 Timothy) Advice to a Young Pastor

Having left Timothy in Ephesus to straighten out some problems, Paul writes to clarify some doctrinal and practical issues (3:14–15), and to encourage him in his ministry. His second letter to Timothy is probably the last letter he ever wrote, and is very warm and personal in tone as he bids his young friend farewell.

☐ **1 Tim. 1:1–20 Greetings and exhortations.**
What things are characteristic of false teachers? How does Paul see his own life as an example of God's grace?

☐ **3:1–16 Appointing overseers and deacons.**
What qualities should a church leader possess? Why should the leader have a record of "managing his own family well" (4, 12)?

☐ **4:1–16 The proper conduct of a minister.**
What does Paul say about "spiritual exercise" (8)? How should Timothy respond if his church members think he's too young?

☐ **6:3–21 "Be rich in good deeds."**
Why is contentment better than wealth ((6–10)? What kind of wealth should we strive for (17–19)?

☐ **2 Tim. 1:1–18 "Fan into flame the gift of God."**
How does Paul encourage Timothy to greater boldness? Why was Paul himself so bold in preaching the gospel (12)?

☐ **2:1–26 Encouragement to faithfulness.**
How can Timothy multiply the outreach of his own ministry (2)?
How should he respond to youthful temptations (22)?

☐ **3:1–4:22 "Preach the Word."**
How important should God's written Word be in Timothy's ministry (3:16)? What words would describe Paul's feelings as he looks back on his ministry (4:6–8)?

WEEK 9

(Hebrews) Jesus Christ Is Greater Than All

If you had been a Jewish convert to Christ in the first century, new in your faith and facing constant persecution and rejection by family and friends, would you ever have considered returning to Judaism? Hebrews reminds Jewish Christians that Christ is the perfect fulfillment of the Law, and that his salvation is far superior to anything the Law could offer.

☐ **Heb. 1:1–2:18 Christ is greater than prophets and angels.**
In what ways is Christ greater than prophets and angels? What very serious conclusions should we draw from Christ's supremacy (2:1–3)?

☐ **3:1–4:13 Christ is greater than Moses.**
What is one striking difference between Moses and Christ (3:5–6)? What does it mean to "rest from our own works" (4:9–11)?

☐ **4:14–5:10; 6:13–7:28 Christ is our great High Priest.**
What about Christ our High Priest should give us great confidence (4:14–16)? How is Christ greater than any human high priest (7:26–28)?

☐ **10:1–18 Christ's sacrifice was once for all.**
What did Christ offer that was better than the offerings of the Old Testament high priests? The earthly priests had to offer sacrifices "endlessly" (1); how often did Christ have to offer his sacrifice (12)?

☐ **10:19–39 Responding in faith to Christ's perfect sacrifice.**
How do verses 22–23 show the importance of responding in faith to Christ's work on our behalf? How is this stressed again in 38–39?

☐ **11:1–40 Even the Old Testament saints lived by faith.**
Faith, not law-keeping, has always been the way to please God (6). At what point in history did these heroes of faith receive remission of their sins (39–40)? How did they receive it?

☐ **12:1–13:25 Final exhortations.**
The Hebrew Christians are encouraged to endure bravely the hardships they may face, and not to let this turn them aside from their faith in Christ.

WEEK 10

(James) Faith and Works

The first converts to Christ soon discovered what has been all too obvious to Christians ever since: Even though we are new creations in Christ, sin remains an ever-present problem. James discusses some of the shortcomings and temptations Christians face, emphasizing that genuine faith will always produce visible results.

☐ **James 1:1–18 Joy amid trials.**
Why should trials and temptations make us joyful? In what way is poverty better than wealth?

☐ **1:19–27 Hearing and doing.**
Why should we be slow to speak? What does it mean to be "quick to listen"?

☐ **2:1–26 Showing favoritism; faith and works.**
Why is it especially wrong for a Christian to despise poor people (5)? How does 2:26 summarize the book of James?

☐ **3:1–12 Taming the tongue.**
What striking images does James use to show the power of the tongue? Have you ever experienced the problems he describes in 9–12?

☐ **3:13–4:12 True wisdom.**
What will be the result of godly wisdom? How does 4:6 answer the problem presented in 4:1?

☐ **4:13–5:6 Advice to the rich.**
What is sinful about the statement in 4:13? In light of 5:3, why is earthly wealth ultimately a bad investment?

☐ **5:7–20 Patience in suffering.**
How should farmers, and Job, be inspirations to us? What are three ways Christians should be involved in each others' lives (13–20)?

WEEK 11

(1, 2 Peter) Rejoicing in Trials

Peter writes to Christians facing persecution and even the real possibility of death for their faith. He encourages them to keep the faith, and points to Christ as their great example of suffering for the truth. In his second letter Peter foresees the problems Christians will face in future times, but also the glory that awaits them with Christ's return.

☐ **1 Peter 1:1–25 Our living hope.**
What is our great hope, as Christians, when we go through trials (3–6)? How should we view ourselves in this present world (1, 17)?

☐ **2:1–3:22 "Growing up in salvation."**
How does the concept of "growing up in our salvation" (2:2) summarize what Peter says in these two chapters?

☐ **4:1–19 Christ's example of suffering.**
Why do non-Christians "think it strange" (4) when we don't join them in sinful activities? If we suffer *now* for Christ, what will our feelings be when we see him (13)?

☐ **5:1–14 Final exhortations.**
How do Peter's letters show that he has taken seriously Christ's charge to him in John 21:15–17?

☐ **2 Peter 1:1–21 Make your calling and election sure.**
What qualities should Christians develop in their lives (5–9)? To what is Peter referring in 16–18? (See Matt. 17:1–8.) Why do you think he mentions it here?

☐ **2:1–22 False teachers will appear.**
What evidence does Peter offer to show that God will judge false teachers? What false beliefs of our own time fit the description of verse 19?

☐ **3:1–18 Judgment and eternal life.**
What does the future hold for those who reject God? What does it hold for Christians? Why is God delaying the final fulfillment of his promises?

WEEK 12

(1, 2, 3 John) *"My Dear Children"*

The aged apostle John writes these very personal letters to Christians he has shepherded in the faith. He shows them the eternal qualities of God, and urges them to make these qualities a part of their lives. John said he wrote his Gospel to help people *find* eternal life (John 20:31). He writes now to help them *know that* you have eternal life (5:13).

☐ **1 John 1:1–2:17 Walking in the light.**
What are some ways that Christians may be "walking in the darkness" (1:6; 2:9)? What should we do if we find ourselves in that situation (1:8–2:2)?

☐ **2:18–27; 4:1–6 Warnings about antichrists.**
From reading 2:20–23 and 4:1–3, does it seem that it would be easy, or difficult, to spot an "antichrist"? How does 4:4 give us confidence to withstand evil?

☐ **2:28–3:10 Children of God.**
What "litmus tests" reveal the true children of God (3:6, 10)? What glimpse of our eternal state of being does 3:3 offer?

☐ **3:11–24 Love one another.**
Where can we find a perfect example of love? How can acts of love help assure us of our salvation (17–20)?

☐ **4:7–21 God's love; our love.**
How important is love as a mark of true Christians (7–8)? What are two other marks of the Christian (13–16)?

☐ **5:1–21 "He who has the Son has life."**
John says we can know we have eternal life if we "have the Son (12). How do we do that? (Read Galatians 2:20, then Ephesians 3:17.)

☐ **2 & 3 John Be on the alert!**
How should Christians respond to false teachers (2 John)? How should we respond to those who teach truth (3 John)?

WEEK 13

(Revelation) Christ and His Church Victorious

As John approaches the close of his life, he is granted a special revelation concerning the ultimate triumph of God and his people over the forces of evil. History, John tells us, will climax with the return of Christ to bring both eternal life and eternal judgment: "Look, he is coming with the clouds, and every eye will see him, even those who pierced him" (1:7).

☐ **Rev. 1:1–19 John sets the stage.**
How does John emphasize the importance of this book (3)? What emotions do you feel in reading the words of Christ and John's description of him? What did John feel, as a first-hand witness (17)?

☐ **2:1–3:22 Christ's words to the seven churches.**
Which churches does Christ commend? Which does he admonish to do better?

☐ **4:1–17:18 Visions.**
(It is impossible in this survey to even begin to explore all of John's visions. Read them with a more complete study guide when time allows. For now, read 4:1–5:14 and join in the worship!)

☐ **18:1–24 The fall of Babylon.**
John sees the complete destruction of "Babylon," his name for the forces of evil. Notice how those who have relied on this evil for their wealth will mourn its end (9–19). (Then read verse 20!)

☐ **19:1–20:15 Hallelujah!**
Describe the scene in heaven as Christ is proclaimed victorious over Satan (19:1–18). Then view the scene at Satan's "campaign headquarters" (19:19–20:15).

☐ **21:1–22:6 The New Jerusalem.**
What will be missing from the New Jerusalem? Try to imagine what all is included by the word "everything" (5).

☐ **22:7–21 "Come, Lord Jesus."**
What important announcement does Jesus repeat three times in these verses? What is John's response? What is yours?